THERE'S A
SOLDIER
AT THE GATE

SECOND WORLD WAR MEMOIRS
OF A TENTH ROYAL HUSSAR

VINCENT A. CROCKER

Note for Librarians: a cataloguing record for this book that includes Dewey Decimal Classification and US Library of Congress numbers is available from the Library and Archives of Canada. The complete cataloguing record can be obtained from their online database at:
www.collectionscanada.ca/amicus/index-e.html
ISBN 1-4120-2651-2

TRAFFORD

This book was published *on-demand* in cooperation with Trafford Publishing. On-demand publishing is a unique process and service of making a book available for retail sale to the public taking advantage of on-demand manufacturing and Internet marketing. On-demand publishing includes promotions, retail sales, manufacturing, order fulfilment, accounting and collecting royalties on behalf of the author.

Offices in Canada, USA, UK, Ireland, and Spain
book sales for North America and international:
Trafford Publishing, 6E–2333 Government St.
Victoria, BC V8T 4P4 CANADA
phone 250 383 6864   toll-free 1 888 232 4444
fax 250 383 6804   email to orders@trafford.com
book sales in Europe:
Trafford Publishing (UK) Ltd., Enterprise House, Wistaston Road Business Centre
Crewe, Cheshire CW2 7RP UNITED KINGDOM
phone 01270 251 396   local rate 0845 230 9601
facsimile 01270 254 983   orders.uk@trafford.com
order online at:
www.trafford.com/robots/04-0479.html

10   9   8   7   6   5   4   3   2

ACKNOWLEDGEMENTS

This book is published as a tribute to my father's memory and as a contribution to the recorded history of the Second World War.

I would like to thank those who have helped in its transformation along the way. To my cousin Sheila Clark, who was originally moved by father's story sufficiently to type it and have it bound as a surprise 80th birthday present, thus enabling it to be more easily read by others. To my son-in-law, Richard Kay, who provided the impetus and enthusiasm to have it published, as well as finding the ways and means. To my wife, Cynthia, for setting it up on a word processor and to my daughter, Helen Kay, for re-jigging and correcting it for publication. To my niece, Bonita Soper, for producing the cover design and arranging the pictorial images shown in the book. Finally, to Richard, Helen, Cynthia and Bonita for editing and checking the final product.

Colin Crocker

Foreword

My father, Vincent Arthur Crocker, was called up in October 1940. He was then aged 32. A Bristolian, he had married my mother, Hilda, in April 1938 and I had been born a year later.

This is the very personal story of my father's war, written in longhand by him after he had retired. His memory was keen and he referred to diaries and letters he had sent my mother, as well as maps and official records. His war took him to North Africa and Italy in the Tenth Royal Hussars. He was abroad from October 1941 until September 1945.

My father was always aware that he was fortunate to survive the war unscathed, when many colleagues did not. He settled back into family life and my brother, David, was born in 1947. He returned to work at J S Fry & Sons until he retired in 1968. He played soccer until he was 40 but continued active participation in local cricket into his early 60's. Despite his love of travel, he never went abroad again.

My parents kept in regular touch with two of father's army pals mentioned in his memoirs, namely George Bull and Alex Watts. My parents lived into their 90's. Father was 95 when he died on 21 August 2003 and his mind remained very active.

Colin V Crocker

2004

CONTENTS

PART I – EARLY DAYS

Chapter 1   Starting Out 1
Chapter 2   England to North Africa 11

PART II – WESTERN DESERT

Chapter 3   C Squadron Technical Store 17
Chapter 4   North African Coast 24
Chapter 5   Cairo 31
Chapter 6   El' Alamein 38
Chapter 7   Tmimi to Tunisia 43
Chapter 8   El' Hamma 56
Chapter 9   Attachment to 1st Army 66
Chapter 10   The Mediterranean Coast 73
Chapter 11   Tripoli 77
Chapter 12   West to Tunisia Again 89
Chapter 13   Atlas Mountains 98
Chapter 14   St Marguerite 104
Chapter 15   Still in St Marguerite 114
Chapter 16   Goodbye to North Africa 125

PART III – ITALY

Chapter 17   Naples 139
Chapter 18   Matera & Gravina 145
Chapter 19   Gravina to Rome 156
Chapter 20   Rome 161
Chapter 21   To Ortona 170
Chapter 22   Moving North 177
Chapter 23   Forli 184
Chapter 24   Pesaro to the Apennines 193
Chapter 25   Rome to Rimini 203
Chapter 26   Northern Italy 213
Chapter 27   Killing Time 224

PART IV – BACK TO BLIGHTY

Chapter 28   The Long Journey to England 239
Chapter 29   Back on Home Soil 244

PART I

EARLY DAYS

CHAPTER ONE

STARTING OUT

October 1940 to September 1941

Bovington Camp

There were quite a number of civilians about my age on the train from Temple Meads Station, Bristol, to Dorchester, the county town of Dorset. Most of us crossed the town over to the Southern Line station, where our numbers were increased. The destination of all was a little station called Wool, this being the nearest rail link to Bovington Royal Army Corps Camp. On this occasion, Army trucks were available to run the expected new intake of recruits up to Camp. On all future occasions the couple of miles had to be covered in the heavy Army footwear so, this day, 3 October 1940 saw the beginning of what was to be five years of Army life.

Most of this intake was formed into No. 68 Squadron for the convenience of all sorts of initial training, not forgetting the square bashing. It was reckoned to take six weeks before a new Squadron was ready to take its place on the big Adjutant's Parade held each Friday morning. After several of these, one was in a better state of nerves to perhaps enjoy a little thrill and the Regimental Band. The two favourite tunes for the Parade and March Past were 'Early one morning' and 'It wasn't the tanks that won the war, 'twas my boy Billy'. There was hardly a thing overlooked in the aim to achieve physical fitness. We were marched off to the dentist now and then; to the Medical Officer for jabs of all kinds and regularly to the gymnasium for athletic exercises.

Soon after No. 68 Squadron had been passed out on the Square, a period of basic training for Royal Armoured Corps followed. This included training such as driving and maintenance of wheeled vehicles, wireless operation, map reading and tank gunnery.

Gunnery training was held at nearby Lulworth, on the Dorset coast, where a gunnery school, ranges and so forth existed. I recall a typical Sergeant Major incident. As was the custom, open Army trucks made the trip over to Lulworth, with so many men to each truck. It was early on a late autumn morning with a heavy frost and a bitterly cold air, but the sky was clear and the sun would soon rise. As some protection from the cold, most were wearing scarves and gloves. The scarves were wound about our necks and covered much of our faces too. On arrival, the Gunnery Sergeant Major had us stumbling quickly from the trucks and instantly on to parade. Then, in his loudest possible voice, he roared forth, "Get those b... scarves and gloves off, there's the b... sun burning yer eyes out".

The last stage in the development of No. 68 Squadron was that an officer, whose job was to grade us into what was considered our best group, interviewed each individual. Each had to undergo the specialised training of that group, and the training periods of the groups were of varying lengths of time. Numerically the most popular groups were those concerned with tanks, so most became tank drivers, wireless operators or gunners. A very few of us, however, were selected to become driver mechanics, fitters, electricians and one only, myself, Technical Storeman. These latter groupings had much longer training periods. In the interview I was asked about my civilian job and the officer seemed impressed that I worked in the Stock & Dispatch Department at J S Fry & Sons, a big reputable chocolate manufacturer. I also disclosed that I once owned a motorbike and knew the names of the engine parts. "You should be just the chap for a Technical Storeman" said he and I was quite pleased about this.

I duly reported to the Technical Stores located some distance from the sleeping quarters and adjacent to the tank park, wheeled vehicle garages and workshop. There was a staff of about seven on the establishment in the Stores, and about four at any given time were trainees. The Stores' operational hours were 08:00 'till 16:30 but there was a lunch break and a short morning tea break.

No. 68 Squadron continued to be housed together in barracks despite the group's daily departure to their own sphere of training. This continued until, having concluded their training, small or larger groups got posted away to join their allotted Regiments and we dwindled down to a very few.

During this time, I became a member of No. 68 Squadron Soccer Team and played about half a dozen games. Evenings and weekends I played much table tennis at one or other of the numerous clubs. There were several NAAFI, YMCA and Salvation Army clubs in the Camp area. Most of my table tennis was played with a pal from No. 68 Squadron and we also went to church services together. These were voluntary services at the little Free Church, held on Sunday mornings. There was a large Church of England Church in the Bovington Garrison and, as my pal was C of E, we sometimes went there on an evening. There was too, the occasional night guard duty, concert parties and the Garrison Cinema to keep us happy.

My period of training at the Technical Stores lasted about 20 weeks, after which a written test and knowledge of spare parts test were passed. By now it was the springtime of 1941 and, having become a Technical Storeman Class III, hopes of seven days' embarkation leave increased. Working at the Stores continued and by summertime a couple of other trainees had passed their tests and we were rather wondering about getting a posting. For about a month, or a little longer, I was moved to run a small store at the workshops over the road. This was a small lock-up place where the workshop tools and equipment were kept. These were drawn out as required, under signature, by the fitters and mechanics.

The only leave allowed was a short weekend or two

and so the 1941 summer sped on. The daily papers (sometimes unable to be printed) gave details of air raids on this or that town, including Bristol. There was the occasional daylight 'dog fight' in the air over our Dorset area, when sometimes the enemy was turned back over the coast.

When, in July and August, I was back in the main stores, it was a nice change to accompany the Sergeant and Corporal a few times in taking a lorry over to Hillsea Ordnance Depot at Portsmouth to pick up stores required. Because of my extended stay at the Technical Stores, I was in contact with several fellow troopers who, having come after me, had done their training stint and passed the exam. One of them was Len Goring, whose hometown was Newport in Monmouthshire. Neither he nor I had as yet obtained a seven days' leave pass and, thinking it was time we did, we both applied together in early September. By mid-week we had reason to believe we were going to be lucky, since our pay books had to be handed in to the main office. This was usual practice so that the leave granted could be entered along with the officer's signature.

Len Goring and I, on the Friday, left Technical Stores after the morning tea break and went to our barracks in order to pack our kit in readiness for a quick get-away to our leave. It was customary for leave passes to be handed out following the normal Friday noon pay parade. Just before noon, however, Len Goring and I received urgent instructions to report to Technical Stores and so made our way down there wondering why. We very soon learned from our Technical Quartermaster that our intended leave would have to be cancelled because we were both being posted forthwith to the 10th Royal Hussars.

The next morning two rather disappointed troopers collected pay books in which seven days' leave had been cancelled. We also collected rail travel warrants and our own kit bags. Thus it was 'goodbye' to Bovington where I had spent almost a whole year.

10th Royal Hussars

We both caught a train from Wool to Southampton and, as there seemed to be plenty of good daylight left, decided to have a quick look around the town. There were, however, very few trains on the cross-country route from Southampton to Swindon, which line served Ogbourne St George on the Marlborough Downs in Wiltshire. We also discovered this route to be very slow and it was a late hour and pitch black when the little wayside halt was reached. We were indeed fortunate to come upon a couple of souls in the village who were able to direct us to the correct campsite. The Guard Sergeant bundled us into the nearest hut to sleep off the rest of the night.

Upon reflection, the twelve-month period at Bovington had shown that my adaptation to Army life had gone reasonably well. Naturally, there were days when the spirit sank low but, on the whole, there were many times of fun, sport and happy comradeship in life at the Camp. I had a most joyous week in the summer of 1941 when my wife and baby son came to stay at Wool and I managed a sleeping out pass for this time. The Technical Staff allowed me to leave the store soon after 16:00 hours most days, so we enjoyed long evenings together. To some extent, this compensated for my being unable to obtain seven days' leave during the Bovington period though, of course, there were several weekends when I managed to reach Bristol, whether with a pass or not. The art of hitchhiking was often helpful to this end.

During our first morning with the 10th Royal Hussars, Len Goring and I had our posting completed when, having been interviewed by the Technical Adjutant, he was placed in Headquarters Squadron and I into C Squadron. I was soon to discover that HQ Squadron carried the main Technical Office and Store and, of course, most of the technical personnel. However, there was one Technical Storeman to each of A, B and C Squadrons.

In less than one day of being with C Squadron, I applied for leave. This led to an interview with the Squadron Leader, Major (the Hon) A B Grenfell, from whom I learnt that the Regiment was very busy preparing to go overseas and that all personnel had already enjoyed seven days' embarkation leave. He was very sorry but time was too short for any leave to be granted!

The next few days saw me caught up in hectic overseas preparations. In the main these were personal matters, such as injections or getting kit bags stencilled in coded letters and numbers, and such things. The Squadron Sergeant Major had me helping out in the Squadron Office along with the Office Clerk, hence I missed out the morning parade and perhaps a few other routine stunts.

About eight days had quickly gone when one morning came a big surprise – the Squadron Leader wished to see me at once. This was no trouble since he was in the adjoining office. The outcome was the granting of 72 hours' leave starting at once. Within a very short time I was walking the road to Marlborough. There was, of course, nothing to indicate that the town was Marlborough, since all signposts, place name boards and such like, had long since been removed as an anti-invasion measure. I had been told it would be "a piece of cake" to hitchhike from Marlborough and so it proved because I reached Bristol with no bother.

What can one say of such a leave, and a brief one at that, all the family and I having the knowledge of my going overseas in mind – didn't know when, didn't know where, didn't know for how long! Later I recall being told, "You left home with a smile anyway".

It was late evening when I did leave home, accompanied by my father and father-in-law, but only as far as Bristol Temple Meads Station. The blackout of all lights caused the city to be very dark indeed but this seemed to be in line with my feelings at the time. The train journey to Swindon was made in complete darkness, broken at times by my fellow travelling servicemen lighting a fag. How I found the way on to the Swindon-Marlborough road I'll never know but, after walking several miles in utter darkness, it was like music to my ears to hear what was undoubtedly an Army truck approaching from the rear. My luck was in! It was a 10th Royal Hussar vehicle making its way back to Camp.

The next day it was disclosed that all tanks and most of the wheeled vehicles with single driver crews had departed for an unknown destination. Not many days later, the main body of the Regiment was on the move. During the day, kit bags and much other baggage had been loaded on to trucks and departed. Late afternoon saw us on parade and, led by the Regimental Band, we marched to the tiny Ogbourne rail station. Many were there to see us entrain and eventually off. These were, without doubt, officers' wives and relatives and many of the villagers.

All through that long dark night we travelled. At first I wrote a brief letter home hoping to find a way of posting it later on. The fellow troopers of the compartment were unknown to me since I had been such a short while among them. There was not a lot of talking anyhow. A few played cards for a while, others wrote and, in the end, most snatched a little sleep. On waking from such a nap, I discovered daylight was breaking and our train had halted at a small junction station. (In later years I proved this to be Carstairs in the Lanarkshire area of Scotland.) Here a kindly porter promised to post my letter (he must have done so). The train journey ended at what we could only guess to be Greenock on the Clyde.

Within a few hours we were transported by trawlers out into the Clyde to board a much larger ship. This ship we soon knew to be H T City of Paris, a merchant ship converted into a troop ship. There were other Units of our Division aboard and, in fact, she was loaded to capacity, or perhaps even beyond, with troops crammed into each and every space. We remained anchored in the Clyde for several days, during which time we had the chance to get acquainted with life aboard. Most slept below decks in the same quarters as the mess tables, by way of hammocks slung each evening at a given time. There were, however, a few biscuit mattresses available for lying on the floor. Late evening on Monday 29 September 1941, lying snug in blankets on a mattress, I became aware of the ship's movement and knew that we were on the move.

CHAPTER TWO

ENGLAND TO NORTH AFRICA

October to November 1941

By early October it became obvious we were part of a great convoy of ships and it was comforting to note the Royal Navy very much in attendance. On the far horizon of both the port and starboard sides, Naval destroyers were patrolling and other Naval ships were deployed amongst the troop ships.

One of our escort ships ejected aircraft for regular reconnoitres. The news, rumour or not, soon spread that the whole 1st Armoured Division was sailing in the convoy and that our destination was expected to be the Middle East. Because of the war situation at the time, this would involve a long sea voyage via rounding the Cape of Good Hope. Also, because of enemy shore-based aircraft, we first sailed west far out into the Atlantic before turning south.

I was still more or less a stranger to most of C Squadron personnel and so life for me was rather lonesome. This seems a strange statement to make as I was on a ship loaded with troops but, nevertheless, it was so. My main buddies, the only ones I had any contact with, were the Squadron Clerk and Len Goring of HQ Squadron, which was located in another part of the ship.

To make this situation worse, I was one of the very

first to become seasick. Actually there was no sickness at all, only very severe pain in the tummy and so I was taken to the Medical Officer. He, it transpired, rather suspected appendix trouble and so I found myself in the Ship's Hospital. Thus, four out of the first eight days at sea were spent in a hospital bed. Two others occupied the compact cabin that served as a ward.

By the time I was discharged from the Hospital, our convoy had turned south and the weather was warming up. There was now a more settled way of life aboard. Space was found for lectures and PT to be held. The Regiment started a library (the books must have been labelled – "Wanted on Voyage") and so I enjoyed quite a lot of reading. Many hours were spent by some of the troops playing cards on the open decks and the old Army favourite game of 'Housey-Housey' was popular. There was always interest in watching the Naval ships patrolling through the ranks of the convoy or spotting the destroyers on the far horizon. Len Goring and I were often together on these days.

The time came when our convoy turned eastwards and day canvas awnings were erected over the well decks to afford some protection from the sun. In a few days we were in calm tropical waters and so sailed into Freetown, a hot and humid coaling station in West Africa. For four days our ship was anchored just off shore, during which time coal was brought on to the ship from the barge-boats manned by native inhabitants. For us it proved to be a somewhat amusing time watching the native 'Bum Boats' trying to sell their delicious fruit to the troops. The fruit was hauled up on deck by means of a fine rope and small basket but not before the 'Boys' had parted with their money. The native inhabitants were also very good divers and would be quick to entertain us when money was thrown into the sea. It was here for the first time that those who normally slept on mattresses were allowed to sleep on the open decks. From here a new sound was heard, which turned out to be the shrill whistle from the little engine that hauled a short train along the foreshore nearby.

Eventually we sailed away from Freetown and turned south away from the African coast and life aboard continued much as before. There was some light-hearted comedy when the Equator Line was crossed and King Neptune and his Court appeared. Many were 'ducked' in a specially prepared canvas pool. One day we were issued with new clothing that replaced the old uniform. This was the Army tropical kit and consisted of khaki drill trousers, shorts and bush shirts. The weather was indeed warming up so the new gear was quite welcome.

In due time half of the convoy sailed into Cape Town. We in the other half, however, passed Table Bay and in a day or so sailed into Durban. After the blackout of England, sailing into Durban one late evening was like approaching fairyland itself. Early morning bathing parades were held at one of the main beaches after which day leave passes were granted during our four-day stay.

The people of South Africa were extremely generous to the troops off the convoys who were on their way to the war up north. With the Squadron Clerk as my companion I enjoyed three days of leave, coming back to the ship, of course, each night. It was a sight to behold all the shops fully stocked up, particularly the great displays of fruit which had been in very short supply at home. Many of the church halls were open as clubs for the troops and supplied all kinds of refreshments.

On our first day of shore leave my chum and I decided to have a real slap-up dinner because meals aboard were not all that could be desired. Our first hour or so was spent enjoying all the new sights and shops. About the right time for dinner we found ourselves outside a large department store that advertised a restaurant on the third floor. Up in the lift we went and soon had selected the best four-course dinner on offer from the menu. You may guess just how much we enjoyed that meal, served to us on a beautiful white lace tablecloth with all the silver-like utensils. On calling the waitress for our bill we were asked, "Are you off the convoy now docked?" and on replying, "Yes", she said, "Then there will be nothing to pay". We were surprised indeed and requested to know why and who would foot the bill anyway. It was explained to us that, although the big store did not advertise the fact, anyone off the convoys who happened to come in for a meal would not be charged. She further explained that the staff of the store held concerts and dances to offset the cost. She requested too that we tell no one about this, at least not until after sailing onwards. This vow we kept.

The other days of shore leave saw us, with several soldiers of another Regiment, entertained through the hospitality of a Mr & Mrs Leadbetter. We had some meals at their home and were taken out sightseeing as well. The Leadbetters had two children, a girl and a boy. Grandmother Leadbetter lived there too. It was the grandparents who had emigrated from Yorkshire, England but the elder Mr Leadbetter had since died. Willie, the son, was about 14 and eager to become an Air Force pilot and said he would love to visit England. One evening our host invited us to join them in a singsong around the piano and one of our renditions was "On Ilkley Moor Baht 'at", which caused the grandmother to shed a few tears. What the Leadbetters did for us was typical of the hospitality of all the South African people towards the soldiers off the many convoys that passed through the ports.

Our departure from Durban was tremendous. Dozens of ships, large and small, set their sirens, hooters, whistles and horns going whilst many people waved, cheered or sang from the dock sides. Apparently it was the custom to give the convoys a right Royal send off.

For about a week we were sailing the Indian Ocean and could not have been far from the east coast of Africa. Eventually we were in the Gulf of Aden and the convoy halted offshore from Aden on 3 November. Ships were sent from here through the Red Sea to Suez one at a time because the port was subject to air attacks.

While off Aden, the Navy ships which had escorted the convoy from South Africa and some from England, sailed up the ranks of the troop ships. Their sailors were paraded on the main decks to receive the three cheers of the soldiers of the troop ships. One of these was the Cruiser Repulse and we were sorry to hear, only a few weeks later, that she was sunk by Japanese action in the Indian Ocean.

The time came for the turn of the City of Paris to move

up the Red Sea and we arrived at Port Tuffick mid afternoon on 27 November. Our Regiment had completely disembarked by the early evening and we were soon all aboard a train. This journey ended at a place called Amirya which proved to be a Base Camp on the edge of the Western Desert not too distant from Alexandria. It was a real desert spot with the sand being mainly soft and dusty and we soon experienced a sand storm.

We were based here in tents. There was a huge tent that served as a NAAFI some distance off and it was a hard plod to get there and back. Somewhere in the area too was a 'Shufter' picture show tent which was a bit of a laugh. Many of the Regiment travelled back from Base Camp to the ports to collect our tanks and wheeled vehicles and any other equipment. Hence our stay at this spot lasted 16 days.

PART II

WESTERN DESERT

CHAPTER THREE

C SQUADRON TECHNICAL STORE

November 1941 to March 1942

The war situation in this area at the time had seen Tobruk quite recently relieved. The enemy was being pushed back and was therefore withdrawing westwards towards Benghazi and also south westwards.

Towards the end of our stay at Amirya the Technical Store of C Squadron became mobile, in fact, an Albion lorry fitted with metal store bins. She was a six-wheeled vehicle and carried other larger spares on the floor and was also fitted with a small workbench. This lorry became a base, a home and a workshop for myself, an electrician, a fitter and two driver mechanics. The Squadron Sergeant Fitter, a Corporal Fitter and a Mechanic had a Bedford 15cwt truck from which to operate and call a home and they always moved and worked in close proximity to the tanks. Other wheeled vehicles of our Squadron (and each of A, B & HQ were much the same) consisted of one Squadron Quartermaster's Store lorry, on which the Squadron's food rations depended, one lorry fitted out for the cooks, one 15cwt Bedford with a water storage tank instead of a normal body and three ten-ton lorries divided between carrying petrol and ammunition.

In operation, the wheeled vehicles moved in echelon some dozen or so miles behind the tanks. Each night, however, under cover of darkness, a small B echelon, made up from each Squadron, moved up to leaguer with the tanks for the supply of food rations, petrol, water and ammunition if needed. They, of course, withdrew as soon as possible and certainly before first light. It was normal practice for tracked and wheeled vehicles to park or stop in open leaguer in daylight. That is, in more or less a circle with 40 yards between vehicles. This was in case there was any air attack. At night it was usually close leaguer for the tanks, if in action, and sometimes for the rear echelon too. This was to ease supplies or to aid movement in darkness.

In mid-December the tanks moved from the Amirya area to a railhead and were transported by train to Mersa Matruh. This was as far as the railway was open at the time. A day later it was the turn of the wheeled vehicles to move. We did so by way of the coast road to Mersa Matruh. On the 16th of the month the whole of the 2nd Armoured Brigade, of which we were a part, leaguered over an area in the desert some 35 miles southwest of Mersa Matruh. In a day or two the Brigade moved off for what was to be a 400-mile trek westward.

Our party on the Albion lorry travelled at the rear of C Squadron, a small section of the whole echelon. The tanks, up ahead, travelled on their own tracks in Regimental groups and in desert formation, centred around Brigade HQ. All vehicles had been supplied with food rations (part of all vehicles' equipment was a pressure cooker based on the Primus principle) and were self-contained with regard to meals, but petrol and water was issued each night. Since our arrival in the desert a free issue of 50 cigarettes a week had been given. These were of an Indian brand called Vs and were soon found to be inferior to English brands; thus, in a short time, they were referred to as 'Desert Players'.

The whole of this long trek by the Brigade was directed by compass bearings. Movement, despite the variance of desert surface, was reasonably good but a number of vehicles suffered broken springs, which were of the old leaf type. There were stops made for brew-ups and lunch breaks but the main meal was always evenings after leaguering for the night.

After a few days the Egyptian frontier was crossed. A wire fence from the coast to deep into the desert, but now having gaps here and there, marked the frontier. Some 20 miles into Libya we leaguered for the night and, in fact, stayed in this spot for a period of ten days. I think the original plan to cut across the desert to west of Benghazi, trapping the enemy in the Benghazi loop, had been dropped because they had withdrawn beyond that point. However, the ten days saw time for maintenance of vehicles, obtaining supplies and resting. It was at this spot that Christmas Day 1941 was spent and the festive fare was bully beef and biscuits with brackish water for brewing tea.

Eventually our trek west was continued and took us past those places whose names may be recalled by the 'Desert Rats' such as El' Gobi, Bir Hamit and Bir Tengeder. This was the route taken until we caught up with the forward troops of the 8th Army.

Our Regiment's echelon came to a halt in a wide desert valley. The only feature was a large wind pump, something like an English Norfolk windmill. This was in the area of Saunnu and we troops soon called the spot 'Happy Valley' – I really don't know why! As we were in a forward area no vehicles were unloaded, the order being "stand by to move any time".

By now most of the troops had grown beards and moustaches and had begun wearing all sorts of odd apparel and headgear. This became the rule of 8th Army personnel on the Western Desert and to a lesser degree in North Africa's other areas. At a later date it was reported that Von Rommel had referred to the 8th Army as 'The Scruffy Army'.

We of the echelon had seen little of the tanks during the long approach march across the desert and they were now in a more forward area. Perhaps our armour would be giving relief to some other. Rommel's forces had withdrawn some miles west of Aquadabia and were holding a line at Aghiela. One evening, about the 21st or 22nd January, our party of the Technical Store lorry was ordered to join that night's B Echelon moving forward to supply the tanks. A few petrol and ammo-carrying lorries from each Squadron, plus S.Q.M.S. lorries with food rations, a water truck and us made up this convoy. We moved under cover of darkness, of course, and in line ahead for close support, with an officer in charge. Our lorry brought up the rear.

Eventually we came to a halt and, after some considerable time, a Sergeant Lumsden contacted each vehicle to explain that this was the compass bearing given for us to rendezvous with the tanks. That the tanks were not here was obvious but it was equally obvious that the enemy must have started something, since there were many gun flashes and activity forward of us and also away to our right. After a long stay at that spot, we were ordered to move forward just a matter of 500 yards. Then we were told to keep quiet and, if possible, rest or sleep, as there would be no further move until first light.

The light of day dawned with a very heavy mist prevailing so that visibility was very limited indeed. More than a further year was spent up and down the Western Desert but we never again saw a morning mist like that. A reconnaissance of the area proved fairly conclusively that enemy tanks had passed through the area of the convoy's first leaguered spot. Our small convoy moved off into the mist, taking care to keep the vehicle ahead of us in view. Some time later, the visibility improved and, as we seemed to be alone, we halted for breakfast.

Of course, normally we would have rejoined the main echelon under darkness and after supplying the tanks with their requirements. However, owing to major action flaring up we were forced into regaining our rightful echelon by other means than a direct route.

After breakfast our convoy moved on and soon picked up a party of men from B Squadron who were on foot, having been forced to abandon their damaged tanks. Some of their personnel were wounded and they were very fortunate to stumble on us. They had been marching north eastwards, away from enemy positions and advised us to do the same and so we headed for Msus. We never did return to Happy Valley.

When in the evening we eventually reached Msus it was to discover, to our joy, the main Brigade echelons leaguered about the area. At last the 10th Hussars' echelon was reached and we ourselves rejoined the C Squadron section. The other 'boys' crowded around to hear our story and we, in turn, were told by the Squadron Clerk of having been reported as missing to Brigade HQ.

The enemy, which had been pushed back hundreds of miles, was now breaking out and forward. After a few days 'standing by' at Msus, the whole Brigade echelons withdrew about 100 miles to Fort Mekili. Shortly after, by the end of January, we withdrew another 80 to 100 miles to the area of Gazala. Here, at this spot each day, remnants of tanks and crews, or perhaps crews only, came back and it was good to see our C Squadron 'Flying Fitters' return in the Bedford truck.

In containing the enemy push for a time, the three armoured Regiments of the Brigade, 9th Lancers, Queen's Boys and our Regiment suffered heavy losses in tanks and personnel. In C Squadron those killed included our Commanding Officer, The Hon. Major A B Grenfell, Lieutenant Graham and Squadron Sergeant Major Bamford.

A defensive line was now being held roughly from Gazala to Bir Hachem. Regiments of our Brigade soon began to be withdrawn in turn to the Fort Capudro area to reorganise and to refit with tanks. It soon became our turn to move back and, once there, a workshop compound was set up for all the four squadrons' fitters, mechanics, electricians and technical store personnel, together with the store lorries.

Fort Capudro area proved a busy time for us. It was a desert spot and the days were very hot even though it was only February and into March. One day we were forced to remain in the store lorry while outside a very severe sandstorm ruled the roost. The canopy of our lorry was sealed down all day but, even so, a thick layer of sand covered everything and our tea and meals were gritty affairs. Most of the wheeled vehicles were given an overhaul and the Regiment was re-equipped with tanks whilst there.

CHAPTER FOUR

THE NORTH AFRICAN COAST

March to June 1942

Along the Coast

Moving about mid-March the tanks, by means of transporters, went forward via El' Adem. The echelons finished up in the Bir Hachem area with the tanks more forward than us. We stayed in this spot for about seven weeks.

To catch a glimpse of us here you would discover our Albion store lorry dug well down into the sand. That was the order here for all echelon vehicles. We also slept in dugout positions called slit trenches, each person having his own trench with a bivouac tent over the top. These trenches were usually some 2ft 6ins deep and besides being a precaution against bomb blast or shellfire, gave more headroom in our bivouacs. We were, of course, in open leaguer here. At this time, the Albion store lorry was a home for Charlie Slark, a Corporal Electrician; Frank Heath, a Lance Corporal Fitter; Jim Cowell and 'Dutch' Holland, two Driver Mechanics, and me as Technical Storeman. This is what I will call 'our party' but, of course, the personnel changed a little from time to time. Some 40 yards from us was the small 15 cwt Bedford truck that was now manned by 'Blondy' Osborne, the Sergeant Fitter; 'Bud' Fisher, a

Corporal Fitter and Bill Howe, a Lance Corporal Fitter. These were called 'The Flying Fitters' by most of us.

This Bir Hachem spot was nothing but sand – no built-up area existed. The Bir in any name in the Middle East simply means a well. A water well is, of course, a very important place in desert country. In fact, there were very few towns or villages in the desert. Some names were given for areas and the Army named places of significance by erecting a stake in the ground carrying a name board. Most of the real towns were along the coast but these were few and far between.

Minefields played a big part in the line being held forward of Bir Hachem-Gazala but the enemy must also have been re-grouping and reorganising after the recent push. For us, at least, the weeks spent here passed off very quietly indeed. One day it was whispered that leave parties to the Delta were to commence. This proved to be true and Frank was the one to go from our party and seven days' leave in Cairo was the ticket. This very first leave party returned after a fortnight and the verdict was that the time in Cairo was OK but the days spent travelling to and fro were something of a nightmare. Frank, incidentally, went sick in Cairo and did not rejoin us until some weeks later.

After dark in this area we used to close the canopy and tailboard of the Albion so we could then have a small interior light. We would then enjoy reading or writing and sometimes playing a game of cards.

It was towards the end of April that we had our next move and it was a backward one, to the area of Gambut some 40 miles east of Tobruk. The following day our tanks, coming together with the echelons, broke the quiet of the area. In a day or two we were all issued with new tropical khaki drill kit so once again cast aside the winter battle dress. On 1st May HRH Duke of Gloucester paid the Unit a visit and inspected the troops. Lieutenant General the Duke of Gloucester was the 10th Royal Hussars Colonel in Chief.

Soon after this, C Squadron was selected to be re-equipped with the new American General Grant tanks, the only Squadron to do so. This tank carried a 75mm gun, a big improvement on the 2-pounder gun of the British Crusader tanks which we had until now been using and which the other Squadrons would still continue to use. The General Grant tanks, however, were less mobile and heavier, and the gun was mounted low in the vehicle instead of in the turret. The turret, in fact, had a smaller gun.

From this Gambut area a second leave party to Cairo was allowed and Charlie, of our party, went. One day, soon after HRH The Duke of Gloucester's visit, an opportunity was given for those who wished to go for a swim. Several vehicles loaded with troops did the trip. A rather long journey ended at Bardiyah. This small town seemed completely empty and its white buildings had been knocked about a lot. The coast here was not unlike Cornwall and the little bay to which we went was delightful. Only a few of us had bathing trunks so most enjoyed a swim in the nude. We returned to our Regimental area by way of the normal desert tracks and when arriving back could all have done with a bath to rid us of the sandy dust thrown up by the vehicles.

Towards the latter end of May we had a forward move

to the El' Gobi area, the tanks being forward of the echelons. It was expected that the enemy would soon attempt a breakout and plans had been made in anticipation. This was achieved by way of several large minefields laid to create what were termed as 'boxes' – it was hoped to catch them in these. Not many days passed before the battle called 'Knightsbridge Box' commenced and soon afterwards our echelons moved further back to the area of El' Adem.

Early one morning from here our party in the Albion store lorry went some miles forward to recover one of our supply lorries that had broken down. The vehicle was towed back and work soon started on the repair. The driver was Alex (Smoky) Watts and he and his vehicle were with us for a couple of days, during which time he shared my bivvy at night. During this period there was enemy air activity mostly at night. However, on a daylight visit by Stukas one of our petrol carrying lorries was destroyed. There were also many other daylight dogfights in the area.

A day or two later we were moved some ten or so miles further back but still in the El' Adem area. However, it was thought the battle was going well in our favour. Nearly a week was spent at this spot and then the echelons were withdrawn from the area entirely and we made our way to Sollum over the next couple of days. For part of this journey the coastal road was used and it certainly was a wonderful roadway, running as straight as a die for as far as the eye could see like a blue ribbon against the yellow-brown sand.

A few miles before Sollum we came to the edge of an escarpment that provided a great view of the vivid blue

Mediterranean Sea and the silver sand of the shoreline, all sparkling in the blazing sunshine. The pass down to the lower level was somewhat tortuous but we made it and our Squadron echelon leaguered right on the beach. The Flying Fitters soon joined up with us there. There were a few days easy time given, so swimming or bathing and playing ball games on the beach was enjoyed. I had a birthday here (17 June) and was lucky enough, as if by chance, for a mobile canteen to turn up, so we had some extra goodies. Tea that day was a feast of fried eggs and bread – quite a change from normal desert diet.

By this time both Frank and Charlie had rejoined us after their Delta leave and, in Frank's case, after his sick spell. Frank had brought a camera back, so our party and the Flying Fitters had a group picture taken on the beach. We also received an extra surprise here of 50 cigarettes each. They were an American brand and each packet was marked 'A gift from your American friends'.

We had not seen anything of our tanks or crews for over three weeks now but it was generally understood that everything was going well up forward. Four days were spent at Sollum and then we had a backward move to a spot called Machifa. Here we leaguered up near the railhead. It was strange to see a supply train complete with barrage balloons attached. There was to be no take-over of new vehicles, however, and indeed we soon moved again, and again in a backward direction towards the area of Fuka.

We were beginning to realise that the enemy had, after all, broken through at Knightsbridge. Our stop at Fuka lasted two nights and we then moved right back to the

Amirya area from where we had started off some seven months before. On the way back from Fuka our Albion had to take a broken-down lorry on tow, so it was not easy going. The weather was scorching so we all travelled on the outside of vehicles wherever possible.

Getting nearer to the Delta, at a brew-up spot we were able to gather a few figs from shrub-like trees. Brief stops for brew-ups on the desert saw one of our party grab a spade and quickly dig a hole in the sand. Meanwhile, another would snatch up a can of petrol and pour a fair drop into the hole. Others would be filling up our Dixie Can (home-made, cut-down petrol can) with water. A match, a flash, a fire, a few minutes, and then the tea was thrown into the boiling water. Milk from a tin and, if lucky, a little sugar would be added. The water would be brackish in any case but the drink was always acceptable.

It was early afternoon when the convoy reached the Amirya area and, after a meal, all received a double pay issue and were allowed to use the canteens, etc. The following morning held a surprise – we were to take over a number of new wheeled vehicles. Our party was to lose our old Albion home and take over a three-ton Ford. We had to strip the Albion of all its fixtures, work bench, store bins, the lot, together with all the stores, tools and personal kit. These had to be refitted into our new vehicle. A further twist to this surprise was that we were ordered to be ready for a move by 14:00 hours. The convoy did move and so retraced its path to Fuka where we slept that night under the stars.

During the following day another move was ordered and so it came about that we retraced our path yet again but the eastward move this time ended up at Alamaid in the area of El' Alamein. A number of days were spent here just standing by and then a move took us much further back to a place named Bir Victoria, a desert spot roughly equidistant from both Alexandria and Cairo. Very soon from here leave was recommenced to Cairo and so Jimmy of our party went with a small group from the Regiment.

CHAPTER FIVE

CAIRO

June to October 1942

Around Cairo

A few tanks were taken over at Bir Victoria and used for training purposes. Some armour of the Brigade, however, was involved in the defensive line established at El' Alamein and so one Squadron of tanks was made up from the Regiment and, with the other Regiments doing likewise, the equivalent was created of one Regiment's armour.

During the evenings in Bir Victoria, lorries were made available to run those wishing to go into Khatatba, some six to eight miles away. At Khatatba a permanent Army Camp stood and we troops would go over to take advantage of shower baths, canteen and pictures. The picture house was a mobile affair set up in a huge marquee tent. A real luxury we all appreciated at Bir Victoria was to have bread available and, furthermore, we could have plenty of jam on it. Indeed, we had jam with almost everything and anything and, in truth, got fed up with it. This jam came in large tins and was a brand made by 'Keiller'. Before very long a little song became popular about the area. These were the words:

Keiller's Jam, Keiller's Jam,
we all love Keiller's Jam,

Pineapple or Apricot,
you can have the blooming lot,
So every night when fast asleep
I'm dreaming that I am,
Bombing ol' Fritz, giving him a blitz
With a load of Keiller's Jam

After several weeks at Bir Victoria it became my turn to enjoy a period of leave at Cairo and 'Dutch' of our party was also included in the group. We travelled in the back of a truck and mostly by the main Alexandria to Cairo road – a decent tarmac ribbon running through the sand. We caught a glimpse of the Pyramids of Giza as we approached the Green Delta. Most of us in the group stayed at one hotel in the central part of the city and, in the main, moved about together. The hotels were made available to service personnel and were mostly booked for bed and breakfast at 25 piastres per night.

It took a day to become used to town life and traffic dodging. Much of our time was spent in one or other of the many services clubs and a firm favourite with me was their ice-cold lemonade. One day some of us took one of the many pony traps for the trip out to Giza to view the Pyramids and the Sphinx. These were very impressive indeed and when one is told the statistics the mind is full of wonder. The large pyramid is about 4,800 years old, stands 480 feet in height and covers an area of 13 acres. It consists of blocks of stone, each one weighing 2½ tons and there are 2,300,000 of them. I personally did not stay long enough to count them!

The leave party of ours was recalled to our Unit after

only four days out of the seven but we never knew why, unless it was that the Regiment had moved.

We caught up with them leaguered at Mariopolis, a spot within a few miles of Alexandria. Only hours after our return we were granted the remaining part of the leave in Alexandria which, being near the coast, was much cooler than Cairo. It is strange to relate, however, that I cannot recall anything about those few days spent in that ancient seaport city.

The Regiment stayed about ten days in the Mariopolis area after my return from this leave. It proved to be rather a worrying time because of the mosquitoes, which plagued us at night. We were mostly sleeping under the stars here and I suffered many bites and bumps all over my face. So there were no regrets when we had the next move to Khatatba itself, where it was a treat to be housed in large tents with a kind of double top that kept the tents nice and cool. The ground area was still sand, of course, but it was great to have the extra comfort and luxuries available. August and most of September was spent at Khatatba and it was a very hot period indeed so it was an added pleasure to enjoy showers, ice cold drinks and big slices of water melon!

The large tent became jointly Squadron Office and Technical Store so once again I worked alongside the Squadron Clerk. Our Sergeant Major now was 'Buck' Jones who also spent much time in the office, including his afternoon siesta, which time I used for writing mail home. In fact my Christmas mail for 1942 was all sent off from there. 'Buck' would often pull my leg about this and would always come out with the remark, "What, writing home again!"

Cairo

On 15 August I joined with a small party of five others to go on a second leave of seven days. This came as a complete surprise. We were run into Cairo by lorry and dismounted at the Station Square. The large and popular Hotel Standard was near and that is where the other five went to book in. However, I chose to go to the same place as previously and so made for the Colonial Hotel. The reason I decided to go alone this time was to select where to visit without the indecision and delays of going in a group. The Colonial was a decent place stay and the Egyptian staff would do anything for one's comfort. Whilst one only booked for bed and breakfast, other meals were obtainable and, indeed, during the seven days I twice had supper served in my room. At this time in Cairo there were numerous clubs providing almost everything service personnel needed, so meals were not difficult to obtain.

Much of Cairo I found to be modern but the older parts, bazaars and Arab quarters were dirty and smelly. There seemed to be many ancient mosques all over the place. The poor of the city looked very poor indeed and the streets were alive with beggars, hawkers and the art-ful shoeshine boys. These shoeshine boys, dressed in only a kind of nightshirt and nothing else, operated in small groups. A couple of these would come up on one's rear and smother the Army spit-and-polish boots with a sort of mud paste mixture. You would then be obliged for their pals to give you a shoeshine at the price of several piastres. One day I was walking near the Ezbekich Gardens when this was tried out on me. They were not to know I had been previously initiated.

I caught hold of the boy's complete shoeshine kit and threw the whole lot over the eight-foot high wall of the Gardens. Needless to say, I made a hasty retreat to the nearby Tipperary Club.

The street tramcars ran with several of them linked together, so giving the appearance of a little train. The cars were shaped like toast racks and had open sides. Locals of every nationality and creed would swarm on these cars like flies, riding or clinging to the sides wherever possible.

The mention of flies, leads one to say that they were always a nuisance. It was usual practice to carry a folded newspaper as a fly swat in the city. Two newspapers were then available to service personnel, the 'Eighth Army News' and 'The Crusader' – both issued free at this time and both of which were quite popular.

I took a ride on the metro one morning to Heliopolis to have a look around. This modern suburb stands near where the ancient city of Heliopolis once stood, the famous 'City of the Sun' called ON by the Egyptians. I spent one day at the Gezira Sporting Club where there were extensive gardens with beautiful green grass and lovely trees offering shade from the burning sun. These gardens and the club were on the banks of the Nile and one had to cross a bridge to reach the entrance. There was an extensive range of tennis courts and a lovely area for cricket matches and, no doubt, that was the reason for my going there since Wally Hammond of Gloucestershire was playing in the game in progress.

On the Sunday I went to my first church service for a very long time. This was at the English St John's Methodist and the text of the sermon was "The eternal love of God passeth all knowledge". The benediction hymn was one of my favourites, "Holy Father, in Thy mercy".

It needed no effort to perspire in Cairo, especially in August, and one was constantly mopping the brow, so it was refreshing to call at one or other of the air-conditioned clubs. Under such circumstances it was really grand to sit sipping ice-cold lemonade and I was doing just that when another serviceman started a conversation. He soon said, "You are from the West of England aren't you?" and so it transpired his home was at Upper Eastville about six or seven minutes' walk from my home in Bristol. He had only been out from England a short time and so we passed away an hour talking mostly of home.

One evening, while at one of the many open-air garden cinemas, the air raid sirens sounded and so the show was stopped and the cinema cleared. I strolled back to the hotel, noticing en-route the efficiency of the black-out which was on, the sound of sirens and that all the busy traffic had been brought to a halt. It seemed to be a case of 'planes passing over or near the city, perhaps on the way to the Suez Canal which was subject to routine air raids.

The several garden open-air cinemas of Cairo were attractive but, of course, their programme could not start until dusk. The seating was always in basket chairs on the ground level. One of the garden cinemas, I believe the one called Diana, was quite near the Colonial Hotel and, of course, at this time of the year the windows remained wide open. So it was a case of lying in bed or, more often, just on the bed listening to the soundtrack until sleep came and, with me, sleeping came easily enough.

I have already mentioned the many service clubs in Cairo so let us take a closer look at one I used often during my brief time in the city. This was the YMCA, Gresham Court, in the road called Soliman Pasha, which was situated in an open court and garden near Soliman Midan. Very centrally placed, this open-air setting with its various facilities was intended as a focal point, a town club for all members of HM Forces.

The restaurant provided a menu of hot and cold dishes, with a snack bar and soda fountain for light refreshments. The reading, writing rooms and lounge were undoubtedly the quietest spots in Cairo. Hot and cold showers were available at a charge of 2 piastres including soap and towel. There were games of table tennis, darts, chess or draughts. Tours and guide services were also a feature. Parties left for places of interest both morning and afternoon, with special Nile steamer trips each Saturday. There was a barber's shop, a curio shop and an information bureau. Dances were held Tuesday and Friday evenings with a recorded concert of classical music on Sunday afternoons. We were indeed fortunate to have the use of such clubs in many towns and cities abroad as well as the simple mobile canteens that turned up out of the blue on the Western Desert now and again.

In due time, our leave party was picked up at the time and place appointed and so we returned to our respective Regiments, still stationed at the desert area called Khatatba.

CHAPTER SIX

EL' ALAMEIN

October to November 1942

The end of the Khatatba period came early in October when we moved some miles towards the Alexandria-Cairo main road. The Regiment had taken over new tanks while at Khatatba, which meant that A & C Squadrons now had the very latest American Sherman tanks. A new reconnaissance troop of scout cars was also a new part of HQ Squadron. In this new area, the days passed quickly since everyone was busy preparing for a move up to the forward positions.

The echelons moved some miles forward to a staging area one day and the tanks, moving by night, joined us the next morning. All vehicles on the desert had always been painted sand colour but now camouflage was used more extensively. Thus the Brigade's tanks went forward one evening from this staging area and the next morning canvas dummy tanks were left in their place. Also, when the tanks reached the forward area ready for the battle they were camouflaged with 'sun shields' to make them look like lorries from the air. The B1 echelon moved in close support of the tanks, as did the 'Flying Fitters'. The day our B2 echelon moved into the forward area was a real scorcher and we were all in shirt sleeves and riding outside the lorry.

Soon, from the staging area, three tracks led to our

forward sector. These were marked and named Sun, Moon and Star. We moved into place by way of Moon track. The vehicles were in open leaguer and for the first time we used camouflage nets. This echelon of ours was positioned a good way to the rear of fighting forces of course. Our store lorry was on a little stump of a hill and we never moved in ten days whilst the battle was on.

The guns seemed to open up just before dusk and made a heck of a noise. Each day overhead there was a regular series of 18 bombers a time, going to and from the enemy lines. Sometimes they would return not flying in formation but coming one at a time very low over our vehicles. Probably there were enemy fighters higher up. We were able to know that it was, in fact, our 'planes that came flying very low because they flew in a certain way, with dipping wings.

These anxious days ended on the tenth day when our echelon formed up ready to move. We eventually moved forward about 10 miles up the boomerang track into which Sun, Moon and Star led. During the night enemy 'planes came over but, in our area at least, only dropped flares which hung like huge chandeliers from the sky.

Next day we were again ready to move any time and, when ordered to do so, one of our lorries was a nonstarter. We remained with our store vehicle so our party could work on this other vehicle. The fault was eventually put right and away we went but we were unable to find our B2 echelon. After covering a few more miles, and being near sundown, we parked up for the night. Next morning the tramp of feet woke us and there was a great column of Italian prisoners walking eastwards.

We had a quick brew-up and snack before setting off to find our rightful echelon, and very soon did. We had, in fact, gone too far the previous evening.

As we came up to them, they were once more on the move so we took up our usual place at the rear. At the first brew-up stop we heard the great news of us moving forward about 75 miles that day. 75 miles, eh! The enemy was on the run. This quick move across desert brought us to the area south of Mersa Matruh and we stayed in that spot for two days.

We of the store lorry, however, went out from there doing a bit of salvaging from wrecked vehicles. Charlie, the electrician, found a small wireless set and got it working within a few days. We also found other useful spares, including a small two-stroke engine with other attachments that had obviously been used for charging up vehicle batteries.

When returning to the leaguering spot, behold there were two Italian lorries. It transpired that the small convoy taking supplies forward to the tanks had captured these and towed them back with them. These lorries were loaded with all kinds of stores and we of our party had a nice folding table from this source.

We saw hundreds of prisoners during this move up, some on foot, some crowded on vehicles but they were all smiling as if glad to be in our hands. They mostly requested water and cigarettes. It was strange about the Italian prisoners, for nobody ever bothered about them. They just roamed about our different Regiments for days maybe, before they would eventually be shepherded together.

The next move forward was to a place on the main coastal road named by the Army and sign-posted 'Charing Cross'. It was some miles west of Mersa Matruh and it was here we found our tanks to be static, having been called out of the chase.

It may be well to make mention of all our tank boys here, for they had done well indeed. They had moved into the forward line at El' Alamein during the night of 20/21 October, had been withdrawn for a rest and taken over other tanks on the evening of 28 October. At that point the Regiment had lost six tanks, which were completely destroyed. Numerous others had been damaged by minefields, etc, but were repairable. After a circuitous night march, the Regiments, indeed the Brigade (2nd Armoured) tanks, were back in the line position by dawn on 2 November. The breakthrough and chase had lasted until 9 November.

The Regiment as a whole stayed in the area of 'Charing Cross' for three days and during this time Charlie had the little wireless working. It was quite a thrill to hear the news over the air from London and that the bells would ring out in Blighty on the Sunday.

Our next move saw all track vehicles loaded on to tank transporters and off went the 1st Armoured Division again. It was a sizeable convoy that travelled west along the coast road, passing through Sidi Barrani and on to Sollum. The 10th Hussars spent the night at the foot of Hellfire Pass, before travelling on the next day to Fort Capudro where one further night was spent.

On these one or two night stops it was usual to sleep under the stars. We moved forward again the next day to El' Adem by way of desert tracks and there our remaining tanks were unloaded and went forward again on their own tracks. We, the echelon, stayed put for a further two days. All the while during this advance, Jim, Charlie and I were seated on the top of our lorry between the cab and body. We saw many wrecked lorries, tanks and guns. The enemy had left much of their material on their flight westward.

CHAPTER SEVEN

TMIMI TO TUNISIA
November 1942 to March 1943

Tmimi

The echelon's next move was by desert track to a very large flat area called Tmimi. This was about 50 miles west of Tobruk and something like a dozen miles or so from the coast. The tank crews soon joined us there, having handed over what tanks were left to the 7th Armoured Division, who had now moved up and were continuing the advance.

The Regiment, and indeed the whole 1st Armoured Division, now faced a period of inaction which was to last several months. These were the months of December, January and February. The stay in Tmimi was quite a happy time for us, although there was some reorganising to do. Also during this time some new personnel joined us. We spent Christmas 1942 here and had a much better time than our first Christmas in the desert.

Being static we were able to make ourselves much more comfortable. For instance, our party enjoyed electric light in our bivouacs and in the back of our lorry. This was the result of using the 2-stroke engine we had for charging up batteries. We had the folding table up in the lorry – it made a nice room when cleared of tool boxes, water cans, petrol cans, shovels, picks, personal kit and bedding, large spare parts and other odds and ends.

We were in open leaguer now and had our legs pulled that if anyone required the Store and Fitters lorry they should "Look for the biggest heap of odds and ends scattered about the deck!" Our new Squadron Leader made an inspection of the area soon after his appointment and, on passing us, said with a wry grin, "The fitters have parked". Charlie, of our party was pretty good at caricature drawing, so this proved a nice subject for him to work on.

It was here at Tmimi that a soccer pitch was made in the Regimental area. Heaven knows where the goal posts came from but the nets were disused camouflage nets and, of course, it was easy to mark out the pitch on the semi-hard sand. We also played with the ball with only plimsolls worn on the feet.

At first, a few troop games were played by our Squadron between 1st, 2nd, 3rd and 4th troop, each of these being tank troop and transport troop, which was the echelon. Our transport troop did very well and I notched a few goals so was chosen to play in the Squadron XI versus A, B and HQ Squadron. Near the end of the Tmimi period I also played in our Regiment team in an away match across the desert somewhere, versus an Artillery Regiment.

During the evenings the lorry tailboard would be shut and the canvas covering closed over so our party would have a few hours of the darkness playing cards, or most likely Frank and Dutch playing chess with the rest of us listening to our newly acquired wireless.

During this static period, as in some of the past static periods, all meals were served by the Squadron cooks who had a specially equipped lorry as their base. The food dished up was somewhat better here with bread being obtainable but most dinners were of stew. A marquee tent was conjured up from somewhere and here we had our Christmas dinner, such as it was. This tent was used during January when each Squadron in turn put on concerts. I went to some and enjoyed the fun, for it was mostly that.

Supporting our Brigade was an Ordnance LAD (Light Aid Department). They had a couple of heavier vehicles fitted with lifting gear and that kind of thing for repair work and for fitting new engines into vehicles. They also had a couple of large store lorries and carried spare parts of all sorts. From time to time I visited them for some spare part or other but mostly for wheeled vehicle springs. Lots of our echelon vehicles suffered broken springs travelling over the rough desert tracks and our fitters would repair some if and when it was possible.

The LAD Technical Storeman became a pal of mine. He was known as 'Taffy' since he came from Bridgend in South Wales. During the Tmimi period I would travel the few miles over to their leaguering spot two or three times a week just to have a little chat. Taffy was always very generous, giving me cigarettes and books quite often. If I offered to pay, then he simply wouldn't let me have them. There was one item I was always glad for him to supply and that was the old Army 4 x 2. This came in small rolls and was used for cleaning small arms gun barrels. Taffy had also acquired a set of Italian hair cutting equipment and so he became my barber – and made a good job of it too!

There was a four-week spell at Tmimi when only a skeleton staff remained. This was because most of the lorries went off to help keep supplies flowing up to the quickly advancing forward areas. Benghazi harbour could not yet be used, so our Brigade's lorries formed a transport column. They ferried up petrol and other vital things from Tobruk or from the railhead to an area near Benghazi. They were nicknamed "The Tobruk-Benghazi Haulage Contractors". Also some of the tank drivers left us to help in the moving up of tanks.

One of my pals returned to the Regiment at Tmimi. This was Alex (Smoky) Watts, a driver of an echelon lorry. He had been in hospital for nearly three months because of an accident at the cookhouse, when a dixie of boiling tea tipped over on to his leg. Some mail was awaiting his return and one of the letters told him of the death of his father. He was excused duties for a while and so spent much of that time with me.

Towards the end of February the enemy was holding a strong defensive line near the border of Tripolitania and Tunisia, called the Mareth Line. Our Division was now recalled to the forward areas, so tank personnel left Tmimi for the Benghazi area to be re-equipped with tanks.

Tunisia

1 March was a big day for us, the echelons. We commenced the long trek up to Tunisia. However, it should be mentioned that Jim, of our party, had now been

transferred to the 'Flying Fitters' and had departed with the tank crews some days previously. Our party had a newcomer to the Regiment named Jack, who was a constant source of jokes and puns. He hailed from Clacton-on-Sea and claimed to have been in the fruit and veg business, so the rest of our party joked that he must have been a barrow boy there.

We were on the move again, as were the wheeled transport of the whole Division. There were something like 1,000 odd miles to be covered. Our Regiment moved the handful of miles across desert to link up with the big convoy and we marched in order – HQ, A, B and C Squadrons. Thus our store lorry was not only the last vehicle of the Squadron but also of the Regiment. In the convoy itself we were somewhere in the middle and there was always the LAD behind us anyway. There was an order of march that laid down a set speed per hour and there was to be a 20-minute halt every even hour for engines to cool and at the same time have that inevitable brew-up. For the complete journey Dutch and Frank were in the cab taking turns at driving, while on the top between cab and body rode Charlie, Jack and I.

The stretch of road towards Derna ran along fairly close to the sea and past Bomba Bay. We were not to see Derna, however, for we took the Martuba by-pass, a decent track that cut out the northern part of Cyrenaica, where Derna and Apollonia were situated. The by-pass, for the most part, ran through an undulating valley, for Cyrenaica was a hilly area, and we saw something unusual for the desert, namely grass and trees.

We pulled into our particular leaguering spot for the

night just before dark and soon a petrol lorry of our Squadron came around so that tanks were topped up ready for the next day. This was the procedure each night for this trip. Our party had somehow obtained a large tarpaulin and we had made it possible for this to be fixed along the length of the lorry near the top. This could be let down to provide a covering like a lean-to tent and so we were now sleeping under this. By the time this was done and we had laid out our beds, the cooks had dinner ready. This was usually hotpot stew but sometimes we did have 'desert turkey' (corned beef). This day we had covered 92 miles.

It must have been well after 09:00 when the convoy really got moving the next morning, 2 March. We passed through some very nice country that day. Some of the land was being cultivated and there were a fair number of small trees and bushes. Also we saw numerous farms along the way and even a few haystacks. Towards the end of that day's run we came down over Barey Pass, a steep and twisty gradient, through the little town of Barey, eventually halting for the night some ten or so kilometres beyond the town. Our particular spot that night was in the grounds of an empty farm building and our day's mileage was 90.

On 3 March our day's mileage was only 81. At first we travelled through similar country to the previous day. Each side of the road and set about one and a half kilometres apart were new-looking houses. Each of these had it's own large plot of cultivated land. These houses were all identical, with an open veranda in the centre and rooms each side and they were all painted brilliant white. Over the entrances of all was some lettering in black, of which we could only understand 'Italian Colonisation'.

Later that morning we descended Tokra Pass. The road down over this mountainous escarpment to a lower plain was a feat of engineering. First of all, as we rounded a bend and came to the top of the Pass, we could see stretched out below a panorama of cultivated land intersected by a ribbon of roadway. Where this met the deep blue sea, looking more directly down, a small town of white buildings glittered in the sun. This was the town of Tokra. The whole scene created a grand picture. We descended the Pass carefully via a number of horseshoe bends with the road one minute going west and the next east. In places deep ravines were bridged and in others there was a drop of many feet from the edge of the road. On the mountainside were two Jerry-wrecked 'planes, looking for all the world like two huge butterflies.

Later on that day we passed through the outskirts of Benghazi. It seemed to be full of troops and wrecked buildings. We leaguered up for the night shortly afterwards, at a spot like a huge car park.

We had not gone many kilometres the next morning, 4 March, when there was a three-hour hold up of the convoy and, as it happened, our party was halted in the little town of Gheminess. We were able to have a look around and exchange greetings with a few Arabs. These Arabs we thought to be of the Sanusis Tribe. The road through the town was tree-lined and Frank, being the brainy boy of our party, tried to find out what trees they were. He did it something like this: – showing money to a little group of Arabs, he said in turn the English words followed by the Arabic words for 'money' and 'tea'.

Then, pointing to a tree he said, "Englasi tree – Arabic ___?" After several attempts Frank succeeded in finding out that the trees were, in fact, eucalyptus. I kept a leaf plucked from one of those trees in that little town.

The Sanusis Arabs here seemed bright and cheerful and with broad smiles would say in their own language that the English were 'very good', the Germans were 'good' but for the Italians they would draw hands across throats and shake their heads. On the walls of some buildings were placards showing pictures of Winston Churchill and some of the King and Queen, together with proclamations printed in English and other languages. Many Arab youngsters crowded around the vehicles and they made a right feast of Army biscuits.

Soon after the convoy had moved on we ran into the old familiar desert land and passed through Jedabia, finishing up the day's run in an hour of darkness with a vehicle in tow. This lorry had run off the road and nearly tipped over down a small embankment. This day's mileage was 91.

The following day was static, given over to vehicle maintenance, so the vehicle we had towed-in was repaired. That night I was called on to do one of my rare duties as night-guard. It passed uneventfully.

On 6 March, the convoy covered 80 miles but there was little to see apart from mile after mile of desert and an occasional glimpse of the sea. We did pass El' Agheila, which was rather interesting since this was the area that the enemy held when our Regiment first did battle on the Western Desert. Next day, 7 March, we did 82 miles but there was just nothing to see but desert, though we did go through one tiny place called Nufilia. What a wonderful roadway was this coast road! True, it was the only road, but it was a really good one and seemingly without end. Of course we did know that far away in the east one end went directly into Alexandria.

Our march continued on 8 March, with further desert country and the road often running over wadis that were bridged. I say "were" because Jerry had blown up all these bridges in his retreat. This meant a series of little detours for us, off the road and back on to it again. We covered 84 miles and passed through Sertie.

The following day, 9 March, we reached as far as Burat on the road but here we turned off and took to a desert track. We must by now have been into Tripolitania. We had not gone far on the track when a C Squadron lorry broke down and so we stayed behind to allow the fitters to work on it. Eventually, however, it was decided to take it in tow. Because of this it became pitch black before we were able to reach the Regiment's leaguering spot. I recall walking in front of our truck with a small torch to pick out the track, since lights on vehicles were not allowed. We seemed to find every other Regiment's spot but our own. However, we did arrive at last and had a belated hot meal before turning-in.

10 March saw Frank and Jack up at first light working on the truck and it was ready in time to move off with the convoy. This day we were told extra mileage would have to be done and so we rattled along at a fair speed over a bumpy and sometimes soft sand track. During the afternoon we came to a valley with quite a ridge on one side. On the ridge top was a very large fort, a square one with a tower at each corner just like the wooden

ones we used to play with when kids. There was a large Union Jack flying from one of the towers. Tucked away in the valley behind the fort was a sizeable town which we discovered was Beni Uid. The town, of white buildings, looked very attractive against the deep red of the sandy ridge. We passed through the little town, throwing biscuits to the children, who were asking for them, saying the word 'biscuits' in understandable English. When halting for the night we had covered 125 miles – good going for what was mostly desert track travelling.

Our next day's journey saw us soon reach more pleasant surroundings. We came to more cultivated land and were soon on a made-up road (but not the coast road). Another town of shining white houses, called Torkamin, was passed and our road became lined with small eucalyptus trees. Our leaguering place at this day's end, 11 March, was practically next door to the large aerodrome at Castel Benito. This was where Winston Churchill had landed some weeks previously when visiting Tripoli for victory celebrations. In the field where we spent that night there were hundreds of wild hyacinths in perfect bloom. 71 miles covered that day.

The first thing we heard the following morning, 12 March, was that a big load of mail had arrived for the Division at the nearby airport, so I was hoping soon to have news from home. The convoy was, however, early on the move, for we had been told it was to be a day of higher mileage. For some distance we travelled by tracks which by-passed Tripoli, though we did catch a glimpse of the city now and again from high ground. Eventually the old coast road was reached on the far side and our progress speeded up. A number of little townships were passed, Suani, Zavia, Sabratha, Zuara, before we came to the Tunisian border. Having done 144 miles, we stayed that night in and around the small town of Ben Gardane. Soon that evening most had received mail and I was lucky to receive five lettercards.

Our trek was completed the next day, 13 March, when we reached the Medinien area in a further 45 miles. Here we of C Squadron were parked up in a large grove of small trees some miles behind the most forward positions. From this spot we could clearly see the distant hills of the Mareth Line from which the enemy had held up the forward surge of the 8th Army.

Here mention should be made of our tank crews who had left Tmimi some days before us, together with the B1 echelon (including the Flying Fitters). Tanks had been collected at Tobruk, loaded on to transporters and had travelled almost ceaselessly by day and night up to Ben Gardane. Here, however, orders came for these tanks to be handed over to the 22nd Armoured Brigade. Our Brigade waited at the Ben Gardane staging area for further tanks. When the main echelon arrived in Tunisia, the tanks were already in forward lines with the B1 echelon a little to the rear. Our echelon party then reached a leaguering spot amongst the fig groves near Medinien.

I erected my bivvy tent here, the first time for a couple of weeks, digging the usual trench. All vehicles remained loaded ready to move at short notice. We remained in this rather pleasant spot until the morning of 18 March when our party was ordered to travel forward to the tanks because both spares and 'fitters' were required for several jobs. We found our Squadron's tanks to be well concealed in wadis and then we reported our arrival to the 'Flying Fitters'. They, we discovered, were now housed in a new vehicle, no longer the old Bedford 15 cwt truck, but a new Whites Armoured Car. This was a good thing since they were expected to be up close to the tanks all the time.

We soon heard that all the tanks of the Division had been out at dawn that morning. It appeared they had moved some few miles across the large open plain and then returned again. It was an uneventful trip and so we all wondered why the armour showed itself to the enemy with such a parade. That day, General Montgomery was about the area.

On the afternoon of the 19th our party returned to the B2 echelon in the grove delivering, en route, a few tank spares to one of our B1 echelon vehicles. The time spent in the fig grove had been largely quiet except for an hour or so after dark when enemy 'planes used to annoy us and sometimes prevent us from hearing the news at 8 o'clock (9 o'clock GMT).

On the morning of 20 March we were given a lecture on the forthcoming push to be started that very evening. It was also made known that a New Zealand Division had started out in an effort to blaze a trail deep inland to come around the left flank of the Mareth Line. We were told they were doing well. The big guns of the 8th Army started up that evening at exactly the same time as they did at El' Alamein. From the grove we watched for a time the vivid flashes of the gunfire.

We spent 21 and 22 March in the grove with the din of plenty of action going on up front. Over our little wireless set we heard Mr Churchill's speech before the evening news on the 21st. He wound up by saying that the Eighth Army was on the move again and wishing them God speed.

About late afternoon on the 23rd came orders that we should be ready to move by nightfall. It was made known that we were about to follow in the wake of our tanks in commencing a left flank movement. The New Zealanders had found a possible way around. Each vehicle, our own included, was to carry an extra 12 gallons of petrol above the standard reserve always carried, which was 24 gallons. Being in the forward area, each vehicle was already self-supporting for meals and drinks, but now we were issued with an extra four days' rations to be kept in reserve.

At dusk our echelon had moved into close leaguer on the roadside ready for the off. In fact, it was about midnight when we began to roll slowly forward by desert road, jammed nose to tail in brilliant moonlight.

Going in more-or-less a southerly direction we reached a place called Faum Tatubuin in the early hours of the morning. Here we left the rough road and turned to the west by way of a track that had been sign-posted 'Two Bar'. After a breakfast stop our journey continued. Throughout 24 March it was slow progress indeed since the sand was soft and the going very difficult, with clouds of dust rising from the rear of every lorry.

CHAPTER EIGHT

EL' HAMMA

March to April 1943

The convoy continued moving very slowly throughout most of the night before halting for a little rest and an early breakfast. In fact, we remained static for several hours, giving everyone a chance to have a look around the vehicles and do any necessary jobs.

Before the move on again we had ourselves another meal and then, once more, followed in the wake of clouds of dust. This day, 25 March, was exceedingly hot but there was no stopping when darkness fell. Charlie, Jack and I snatched some sleep in the lorry but were awakened by much talking with our vehicle at a standstill. We soon learnt that several of our Squadron lorries had missed the way that the others had gone. Actually it was about the eighth vehicle of the Squadron that had gone wrong and, of course, the remaining ones, back to us at the rear, had been following them.

We all held a bit of a pow-wow and decided to turn back to endeavour to pick up the correct track. Because there was no clear track over this area of desert, all the vehicles of the Division had spread out with each Regiment picking out what they thought to be the best way. Consequently there were dozens of vehicle track marks and we turned back hoping to possibly pick up the ones of our own vehicles.

We had only re-traced our steps a mile or so when our lorry became firmly stuck in a bank of soft sand and, being the rear vehicle as usual, we found ourselves alone. We set to with shovels in an effort to dig the truck out. It was about 02:00 and, luckily for us, there was a moon. The moon in this part of the world always seemed much brighter than at home. Maybe that was because in a place like the desert there are no other lights.

Well, after much hard labour, we only succeeded in burrowing the wheels further in to the sand. Charlie lost his patience, then his temper, and then Frank became 'browned off', suggesting that we kip down until daylight. However, with the aid of a couple of large wooden blocks (like railway sleepers) that we had amongst our tools and kit, we did eventually get free. It should be noted that a recent addition to each wheeled vehicle's equipment was the sand channel. This was made of rather light corrugated metal about six feet by two feet in size and was carried on the sides of each lorry body. It was an aid to help in soft sand but when wheels became firmly and deeply burrowed, we found they so easily bent up. Well, we had at last got free from this situation but now as to which direction to go for the best, we hardly knew.

In the end it was decided to stay right where we were and try to get some sleep until daylight. We had indeed acted wisely because we were awakened at dawn by much noise and shouting. This was none other than our Squadron echelon passing quite nearby. Our party made a rushed move and very soon we were in our rightful place at the rear of this section. This day, 26 March, the sun blazed down and the going was not very good. There were several extra stops when some vehicles overheated and they had to turn to face the wind to allow the engines to cool.

Towards mid-day we had another new experience for we drove through a huge swarm of locusts. The air was literally black with them. Riding on top of the lorry behind the cab, Charlie, Jack and I had to beat them out of the way with our hats. We also once again experienced a sandstorm, so when coming to our eventual leaguering spot we all looked like we had been pulled out of a sack of flour.

This spot was on the edge of a large plain which seemed to run through a gap between hills towards El' Hamma and the coast. We remained loaded and ready to move at a moment's notice throughout the 27 and 28 March. In fact, everyone was very watchful during this period. We knew our tanks were up somewhere in the gap fighting through to El' Hamma but it was thought that the enemy, if strong enough, might swing some forces from the Mareth area round over part of the ground we had already travelled and so box us in. However, we were not to be cut off in this way and it was comforting to see the RAF overhead quite frequently flying forward to carry out their raids. In contrast, there was a complete absence of Luftwaffe.

On the morning of 29th we heard of our tanks being near to El' Hamma and around mid-day the echelon moved forward – a move of 15 miles – seeing en route plenty of wrecked guns and vehicles. Later that day we heard that both El' Hamma and Gabes had fallen but it was not until the wireless news on the following night that we heard that the left flanking movement of British armour around the Mareth Line had been a great success for they had taken El' Hamma and thus caused Rommell to pull out from the Mareth positions. It was the force that came up the coast through Mareth who had chased Jerry and had taken the town of Gabes.

This day we had moved forward only one mile but on the 31 March we moved four or five miles through the Oasis El' Hamma and leaguered at the far side, near kilometre stone 36 on the Gabes road. On the other side of this road was quite an extensive airfield. The echelon was in open leaguer here and we all erected our bivouac tents over the top of the usual slit trench, otherwise vehicles remained loaded. From this spot one could see another range of hills in the distance. In fact the situation was like being on a plain, such as the Bridgwater flats in Somerset looking away to the Mendips, though there was not the vegetation of that area of course.

Pockets of resistance were in those hills so I think the echelons were held back somewhat. We were static during the first four days of April, during which time gunfire was often heard. One day Stukas strafed the road nearby resulting in two lorries going up in smoke. They were not our lorries however.

On the morning of 4 April, we of our party were chatting at the rear of our lorry when suddenly there came the whine of shells. We all fell flat to the ground as one man. The shells burst about 120 yards away but within the area of our Squadron leaguer. Needless to say, we took to our tin hats and slit trenches but soon the shells were ranged on the airfield across the road, so we calmed down. The same thing happened again in the evening, so we then thought the first few shells that came over were used in finding the range of the airfield and we, of our Squadron, must have been in line with that. It seemed that the enemy had a few long-range guns up in those hills.

The morning of 5 April saw Jack and me up first as usual. Next up, much to our surprise, was Dutch, for he was inevitably last, so we were pulling his leg about it. I was shaving at one side of the lorry tailboard and Dutch was doing likewise on the other side, when the whine of shells came once more. The three of us dropped to the ground within a few yards of each other and a shell burst quite nearby. When I looked up I saw Dutch was bleeding badly from the mouth. I shouted to the rest, "Dutch has been hit" and tried to help him while Jack dashed away to fetch a small 15 cwt truck in which to run him to a light field ambulance. The Regiment's own Medical Officer was always up with the B1 echelon at such times.

Frank and Charlie were dressed in quick time and it was they who went off with Dutch. Frank returned sometime later to gather up Dutch's kit and to take it back to the ambulance centre. Returning several hours afterwards, Frank and Charlie were able to tell us they had seen Dutch with his head all bandaged up and one arm in a sling. We did not know that his arm had been hurt. Frank had learnt from the RAMC officer that Dutch was to be flown to a hospital in Tripoli. It was also discovered that shrapnel had gone through the cab of our truck in several places.

During the afternoon the echelon moved back towards El' Hamma about a mile. Here Alex Watts came on to our lorry as driver in place of Dutch. At El' Hamma there was a hot spring and we were allowed in for a jolly good wash down. El' Hamma was a small Arab town of mostly low-roofed houses in a sort of white sandstone, or that is how they appeared. Some of these dwellings seemed like stables and, as in all Arab quarters, there were camels, asses, chicken, goats and goodness knows what, all around the yards and doorways. The town was tucked away amongst a plantation of tall palm trees.

At dawn the next day, 6 April, a push started to sort out the hill positions of the enemy. Our guns were giving them big licks most of the day and the Royal Air Force was most active too. Also, the following day, there was increased air activity but the guns were now silent. Alex and I were sharing a bivvy now and we had long conversations together at this time when I learnt much about his past life.

Our move from this spot came at first light on 8 April and we travelled by track in a northerly direction from El' Hamma. We understood it would be about an 18-mile move but this turned out to be 50 miles, so we supposed things were going well. We moved off without having a breakfast and it was nearly 14:00 before a break was made. The trip took us across the plain and through a steep, long pass amid the hills and here we saw a large number of prisoners. One party appeared bearing a white flag held aloft. This day's move ended in an hour of darkness but Alex and I still put up the tent and had a good night's sleep.

Next day, 9 April, we had another forward move, passing along tracks made through extensive stretches of wheat or barley. There was much more greenery and cultivation along this coastal plain of Tunisia. We even passed a large inland lake and later on crossed a single-track railway. This rail track was narrow gauge, which we thought to run from Sfax on the coast to somewhere inland. Late afternoon a few enemy 'planes dived out of the sun and strafed our convoy. Luckily for us their dive took them further forward than our Squadron but several of the A Squadron boys were wounded. Strangely it occurred right where the convoy turned off the track to leaguer up in a sandy scrubland field.

The convoy remained static next day but our party were ordered to go out to a tank that had broken down. This tank was only about five miles forward and Frank and Jack set to work and in the end made the engine service-able. We wondered how the 'Flying Fitters' had passed this tank. We returned to the leaguering spot in time to prepare ourselves the usual evening cooked meal. During that night enemy aircraft were busy. Flares were dropped and bombs fell some distance off.

On 11 April a short forward move of a dozen or so miles brought us to another fresh leaguering spot, one that was close to a rather good road and near kilometre stone 72 from Sfax. We were fortunate here to find a number of slit trenches nicely dug so all that was nec-essary was to put up our tents over them. Alex, who had been our driver for several days, had to leave us that evening, going as second driver on a supply petrol lorry to the tanks.

Next morning (12 April) came news that Sfax had fallen. During that afternoon the echelon moved out and forward once again. However, our party of the store lorry had been issued with a couple of day's food ration because we were to remain behind to support the LAD. This was a busy time with the fitting of several new engines to lorries that had become 'tired' in the long haul forward. Having little to do myself, I prepared and cooked the meals for our party.

Two days later (14th) our party pulled out from the LAD in the late afternoon and went forward some 20 miles. We thus came to a spot where we discovered the echelons and tanks to be together in a large olive grove. It was the first time the Regiment had been together since leaving Tmimi in February. Pulling through a gap in a cactus hedge, the first group we caught sight of were our staff of the 'Flying Fitters'. We were pleased to see them because for some days there had been rumours of them being missing. Of course, we stayed and chatted, finding it was true that they had been missing from the tanks but only because of a breakdown of their armoured car during the latter stage of the forward rush. It seemed they were out on the 'blue' for a couple of days before making themselves mobile again. Perhaps it was for this reason that we of the store lorry had been called out to aid a tank on the 10th. Then, in exchange, we had to tell 'Blondy & Co' the story of Dutch, how he had been wounded and had we heard anything of him since? Many were the stories and tales heard on coming together like that after a period of action.

A little bit of scouting amid the perfect rows of olives and we found a spot to park not far from the cookhouse lorry. Soon we learnt that there were some tanks and crews not present. These, at such times, became scattered and could be found either at Brigade workshops way back a bit or at Divisional workshops back even further, having fallen out owing to major breakdown. They soon should have been coming along with tanks repaired or with new tanks perhaps or, at least, with tanks made serviceable. These various workshops kept moving forward just as we did. Sometimes tank crews could be away for weeks. If vehicles were not obtainable they might go to a depot where crews were held in reserve and they could even, for a time, become attached to another Regiment.

There was one major event of the war that I should mention now, since it had a bearing on our 1st Armoured Division's future activities. The Americans had joined in the war some time ago and a Force containing British and American troops, known as the 1st Army, had made a landing in Algeria. These troops had been advancing into Tunisia from the west, creating another front line for the enemy to defend on their north and west flanks.

Another item, a humorous one, dates back to our time in Tmimi. We stayed there for nearly three months and during that time many of the 'boys' had got for themselves some egg producers, by way of chickens and not a few cockerels – maybe to provide some future tasty dish. These had been acquired by some hard bargaining with the many wandering Arabs. During the latter weeks at Tmimi many of the areas around the lorries were looking something like poultry farms. Wooden boxes served as nests, while in some cases camouflage nets served as chicken runs. When we moved and just prior to the dozens of moves since, it had created many laughs watching the 'boys' rounding up the birds. This Arab breed of chicken looked small and thin compared with the English type and the eggs were meagre things.

Most of these birds had survived with the Regiment to reach this leaguering spot in the olive groves.

We remained static for three busy days and my pal Alex came over to my bivvy for a chat of an evening. A couple of C Squadron lorries had been evacuated after breakdowns during the way up from Mareth and so, on 15 April, I drew two brand new lorries from Technical HQ. One of these had to be handed over to Alex. Another driver came to join our party on the technical store lorry. He was George Bull.

CHAPTER NINE

ATTACHMENT TO 1ST ARMY

April to May 1943

We heard that our Division – 1st Armoured Division – was to be temporarily attached to the 1st Army for the final offensive in Tunisia but it was clearly understood that the Division would return to the 8th Army afterwards and we were all pleased to know that.

At dusk on 16 April we took our place as a Regiment in the Divisional Convoy moving westward, for we would have to complete a huge inland arc to get round. We soon reached a tarmac road and although it was quite dark knew it must be the Sfax to Kassiren road. Our party, riding in the back of the truck except for George and Frank who were in the cab, managed to keep awake until passing through the small town of Kassiren and then fell asleep. I am not sure if it was Charlie's or Jack's leg I used as a pillow, anyway the three of us were soon in the 'Land of Nod'.

It was just daylight when we roused ourselves to realise the vehicle was still moving, so we lay where we were until a halt was called. This proved a long break when we were able to wash, shave and have a good breakfast. We were still on a decent roadway up amid the hills and as our journey continued we saw many small fertile valleys, each with a collection of white farm buildings with red tiled roofs, windmills and trees. A mountain stream was quite an attraction to us all, like a pearl necklace displayed amongst common bric-a-brac. Another unusual sight to us were large birds which we took to be storks or cranes in flight and some on huge nests perched right on the top of high trees. Then we also saw 'The Yanks' – quite a number of them belting along in jeeps.

Soon our travelling brought us from the hills on to a large plain but in the distance we could see further hills and just discern the white buildings of a large town. It looked as if the road ahead led up to that town, so we hoped there would be no turn-off. There was not and, passing through, Charlie said, "It looks a typical French place". He should have known, since he was with the Regiment in France for a year before evacuation. The town was La Kief and the inhabitants who were in the streets gave us the 'V' sign as we passed.

Onwards from here we passed many 1st Army vehicles on the road. Their lorries, painted black and green, stood out in considerable contrast to our own. The 1st Armoured Division vehicles of all types still had the desert sandy yellow-brown camouflage. We saw that the 1st Army chaps wore tin hats all the time and that each vehicle had an anti-aircraft machine gun mounted on the top. I don't know what they must have thought about our vehicles! Our echelons gave up this practice some time ago and our store lorry's gun was in its box under a load of kit in the body of the vehicle.

1st Army troops who stood about from place to place with blancoed belts and gaiters gave their sandy brethren a cheer of welcome. Our particular Regiment was, per-haps, not currently living up to its reputation as 'The

Shining Tenth' since it must be admitted we were not quite worthy, what with chickens clinging to vehicles and all the various other trappings collected by the Desert Army.

About 50 kilometres beyond La Kief we leaguered up in a beautiful little valley with wooded slopes, near a village called El' Krib. This was on the afternoon of 17 April and we remained there during the 18th, 19th and 20th. It was a busy period for me and I seemed to be on the go all the time. In the first place, paint had to be spirited up from somewhere and paint was a Technical Store commodity. Dark green was the colour now in demand in order to camouflage the vehicles for this more fertile area. There was a flap on at the Regiment's Technical Headquarters and the Technical Sergeant Major, named Dobbins, had us rushing about in trucks to numerous Ordnance Departments. In the end, we Storemen of A, B, C and HQ Squadrons managed to obtain what we needed. However, paint brushes were limited, so each group had to take turns with their artwork.

On the 19th I was instructed to accompany six C Squadron tank drivers to an Ordnance Distribution Centre to pick up six new tanks. I asked Alex if he would transport us in his truck and so we set off for La Kief where this Centre was located. On reaching the place we learnt that these six tanks had been forwarded to Field Ordnance situated only a few miles from the Regiment. We travelled back and found this place after a little bother and eventually came away with these vehicles, each of which I had to check over regarding armament, kit and tool equipment. Further, I had to sign a paper for the receipt of these tanks and also make a report back to our Technical

HQ. These new tanks brought the Regiment up to full strength armour-wise and were, of course, in the new camouflage colours. There was also a trip out to obtain additional tank spare parts but the most time-consuming job of all was travelling over to our own Technical Headquarters to collect sets of new tools, kit and some gunnery equipment, all of which had to be distributed to the twelve individual tanks of our Squadron.

One evening after dinner, George and I managed to find the time to take a stroll up one of the wooded slopes and found there were many tortoises about. We brought a young one back with us and named it Joey and it stayed in the company of our party for several weeks. Good job there were no tortoises in the desert for they would never have kept pace with the 8th Army!

At first light on the 21st the echelons moved out, our tanks having left the area at midnight, and we travelled 30 kilometres or thereabouts to a forward area. On 22 April, the forward B1 echelon moved further up to be nearer the tanks but we, in B2 echelon, remained static. Early morning of the 23rd, our echelon moved several kilometres forward into the cover of a grove. Here I erected a bivvy and spent most of the day writing letters home. It transpired I was not to sleep in the bivvy, however, because a later order at 21:00 caused us to move into close leaguer – that is vehicles lined up nose to tail. This was usually done to make for an easy move during darkness. We did eventually move forward slowly about a dozen kilometres, starting at 02:00.

On arrival at this new spot very early in the morning, we laid our beds out in the open and were able to snatch some sleep. Before breakfast, orders to open leaguer came, so our Squadron vehicles had to cross a wadi at one spot and park up in a grassy area on the other side. During the day I dug in the still sandy soil a double width slit trench because Alex, parked not too far away, wanted to share the bivouac. There was considerable air activity this day, 24 April. On the 25th, Alex had to take his truck of ammunition up to B1 echelon and stay for a spell.

26 April found us remaining static but there was a fair bit of gunfire going on. We learnt that our area was in the general Medjez El' Bab region but somewhat south of that place. Forward of us the enemy held strong positions in the high hills, one of which had twin peaks. Near at hand was a large salt lake called by our troops 'Sugar Lake' and this, of course, hampered movement for our chaps on this sector of the Front. So it seemed we might be in our leaguering place for at least a few days more and we were, for even much longer, as you will discover.

That night enemy 'planes were over and bombs were dropped. Some landed in our Squadron area making big craters in the ground but no damage was otherwise done. Next day there were many flights of our bombers, usually 24 at a time, going to and coming from enemy-held areas. Our fighter 'planes were often in action too. On the 28th all this was repeated, so it seemed we were always looking upward during those days. Once a couple of Stukas crept in low over the hills from our rear, flashed low over the tops of our vehicles but did not drop anything or even machine-gun us. They were scurrying in the direction of their own lines and safety.

In the early evening we were attracted by a flight of our bombers because, instead of passing over, they circled above our area several times. They then went a bit further out, turned to make a low run in and plastered bombs over an area from echelons to tanks. We saw the first aircraft drop its load so we quickly retired to our slit trenches while the ground shook. When it was all over we could see that the nearest to us was almost half a mile away over a small ridge. The bombers bore the American White Star but we didn't know if it was the RAF or the American Air Force flying them.

Mistakes happen at times, I suppose, but I should imagine they must have realised something was wrong as no guns opened up at them. There were plenty of our Ack-Ack guns in the area with a couple near to hand. Our Division and plenty of the other 1st Army vehicles were quite thick in this area, so some damage must have been done. A couple of ambulances from a nearby Field Unit were seen to dash away up the track leading over the ridge. That evening Alex returned from the B1 echelon and shared the bivvy.

We remained in this spot from 29 April to 8 May. For me it was an easy time with only a return of 'Vehicle State' having to be taken to Technical HQ each day, so I managed plenty of letter writing. Charlie had the wireless set going well but enemy 'planes had a habit of coming over just around Blighty News time at 21:00 (20:00 our time). However, we overcame this by moving the set on to the tailboard of the lorry and raising the volume, so we could hear most of it from our slit trench bivvys. These enemy 'planes used to drop 'crackerjacks', a device that exploded just before touching the ground. However, the raids did not last very long.

Occasionally some of our party would take a stroll after evening dinner through a cultivated part where wheat, barley and poppies grew. There were plenty of tortoises about and more than a few partridges.

Around our breakfast time on 7 May a flight of 80 bomber 'planes, making towards the Tunis area, caused some excitement and we watched their return a little while afterwards. Later in the day we heard that the suburbs of both Tunis and Bizerte had been targeted. The evening brought several hours of rainfall – it was the first rain we had seen for ages.

CHAPTER TEN

THE MEDITERRANEAN COAST

May 1943

8 May dawned with an early order to be ready to move from 09:00 and so it was a day of stand-by because we did not move until nearly 17:00. The move forward was around 18 kilometres passing en route both 'Sugar Lake' and the Twin Peak Hill. We halted at a spot on the plain between very high hills and remained there in close leaguer for a day and a half. This was because we were in a cleared lane through a heavily mined area, so stayed in line ahead. During our time here we saw a number of cattle and horses blown sky high. We suppose they belonged to the farms around. The poor things would wander about and we, watching, expected every move to bring a bang.

The next move came at 14:00 on the 10th and was only of eight kilometres, mostly covered on a decent road. Here our echelon parked up near a large farm and out-buildings. Word had circulated that Tunis and Bizerte were in Allied hands and that fighting here in North Africa was probably drawing to a close. That evening everyone was in a happy mood and to make the 'boys' more cheerful, French-speaking people at the farm supplied plenty of free wine.

From the weather viewpoint, the next day was glorious and early on George and Jack received a call to go up to B1 echelon to take over a captured German workshop lorry. In the evening we were able to sit in comfort inside the truck with the lights on. The wireless included a programme of Jack Payne's Orchestra playing 1935-42 favourites.

Next day, 12 May, we had a first-light move forward of 24 kilometres, all on good roads. We passed thousands of prisoners en-route. At one place 'Movietone News', or some such people, were taking pictures and we believe our lorry was filmed as we passed by.

Our new leaguering spot was on high ground in the hills where we overlooked a plain, the distant blue Mediterranean and the white buildings of the Tunis suburbs. It was a delightful situation. Our stay here lasted three nights and the main memories for me were as follows:- Alex, now a true pal of mine, had suffered toothache so went to have a tooth removed. We had a payday, only the third that year for me. A few of our party went out salvaging and came across a German Ordnance dump. Most of the stores were smashed up – wicked to see it. I found a very good copy of the book Mein Kampf but it meant nothing to me as it was, of course, in German.

On 15 May we moved up to join our tanks and B1 echelon at a place near the small town called Sollum. This town was about 12 kilometres from Tunis, out south on the Cap Bon road. After the move George and I joined a party allowed into Tunis for the afternoon and evening. We thought the city was a dead-alive place but, of course, it had seen a change of occupational troops only about a week before and there was hardly a shop open.

The Regiment stayed in this area for a further 12 days when everyone had, more or less, a free and easy time. We always seemed to have our truck full of friends during the evenings. It created plenty of chat and fun but the real aim was to hear the wireless and, in particular, the London 21:00 news. Some days I joined a truck or two running the 'boys' to the nearest beach for bathing. Swimming in the blue Mediterranean was always most enjoyed, with or without bathing trunks. Other days I stayed quiet and caught up with my writing. Fortunately, I received plenty of mail from my wife, family and friends, some of which came from other war areas; therefore I could always spend an hour sending back my news and good wishes. One evening George and I went with others to a concert show at the Queens Bay area, presented by a French party. It was midnight when we got back.

There was one day when Charlie and Frank went to Tunis while Jack, with George, went off salvaging. Being left in peace and quiet, I took the opportunity of giving the store bins, their contents and the interior of the truck a jolly good spring-clean. The salvagers arrived back from Cape Bon with a smashing German caravan in tow. It certainly was a lovely job, being very long and standing on eight wheels. From the interior, we believe that a German photography unit may have used it but in no time at all it became C Squadron office.

On Empire Day George, Alex and I went to Tunis and found it had bucked up no end. Many of the shops and a big open market were in full swing and we were able to buy meals and drinks of all kinds. The inhabitants of Tunis were a mixture of both Arabs and Europeans. In the evening we went, after queuing, to the Theatre Municipal for the very first ENSA show to be held in the town. It proved to be a very posh theatre with two balconies and a gallery, seating nearly 2,500 people. The artists in this variety show were all English and the Tommies and a few Yanks present fully enjoyed it.

There was one point of interest at a large junction where the road into Tunis left the coast road. Here stood a very large signpost with numerous arms of direction. Pointing up the way we had come were at least seven arms of the post, one above the other. The lower arm simply stated La Cairo 3,000 (odd) kilometres. Our C Squadron tanks had done well indeed travelling through Tunisia without suffering many casualties. Squadron Leader Major Ford-North had accepted the surrender of many German officers and men near Crombolia.

26 May saw most of us sorting out and packing our vehicles in preparation for yet one more move. The fitters were busy working on some of the 'tired' vehicles and also on some of the captured trucks. All these enemy vehicles, however, were supposed to be handed over to the 1st Army Ordnance Department prior to the Regiment's move but as our vehicles and lorries, in the main, were in poor shape we were allowed to keep some of them in the end. One such vehicle was powered by a big German diesel engine called a Hanamac, which our Squadron had 'come by' for the sole purpose of towing the caravan-come-Squadron office.

CHAPTER ELEVEN

TRIPOLI

May to July 1943

The move, due to start next day 27 May, would take us way back east to the area of Tripoli, an 8th Army area of course. The tanks that the Regiment finished the campaign with were loaded on to transporters and, I believe, moved one day prior to the echelon vehicles. Our trucks departed from the Sollum leaguering place at 08:00 but 'Blondy & Co' of the Flying Fitters were still trying to get the Hanamac roadworthy. They were therefore left, together with the caravan and their own armoured car, to follow on at their own speed when ready to do so. Our party on the store lorry became the rear vehicle of the Regiment as per usual. Also, as usual, we knew LAD would be travelling behind us.

The convoy took the coast road southeast, passing Crombolia and later through Enfidaville. Soon we left the coast road and took a road going right and thus bearing slightly inland. After a quick lunch stop we were mobile again and later passed the low white buildings of a small town. This turned out to be Kairouan, the Holy City of Tunisia. Soon afterwards we leaguered up for the night's stop.

Next morning, 28th, breakfast was taken at 06:30 and we moved off at 07:00. The cooks' lorry was now providing meals. We were to have a bit of rough riding because, turning off the road, our way was along poor, bumpy and dusty tracks. A tiny place called Sidi Ammo was passed and then came a lunch stop. Moving off, our way was through an Arab village with the name of Tescga and later we rejoined the coast road at Matrath.

One mile beyond, the convoy halted for refuelling and we had no sooner started moving again when our store lorry suffered a blown tyre. The weather was very hot and the wheel movement also created heat, so tyre pressures rose considerably. During the refuelling stop, George had been around our truck testing and adjusting the pressures but all the same we had one that burst. We were not the only ones, for it seemed a common complaint up and down the convoy. Our spare wheel was soon put on but the convoy was not caught up until we found them leaguered for the night a few miles before Gabes. The day's run was 163 miles.

29 May, reveille and convoy move off was as per the previous day but we stayed with several trucks that were non-starters. The fitters were fully stretched. There was no doubt that some of our older vehicles were on their last legs. They had been to Saunnu and back in 1942 and had come from the Cairo area to Tunis in 1943. This was in addition to running to and fro fetching and carrying the various supplies. Anyway it was nearly 11:00 before we were able to move away and even then we had one lorry on tow.

Progress was very slow and, making a lunch stop at 13:30, we had passed through Gabes but done only 32 miles. While halted for this lunch break, who should we spy coming along but none other than the 'Flying Fitters' armoured car, followed by the Hanamac and its trailer caravan. They did not look unlike Bertram Mills' Circus because of tents and tent poles and other bulky kit tied up on the roof of the van. On spotting us they stopped. Sergeant Fitter 'Blondy' had a look at the troubled truck, said what he thought was wrong and moved on. Frank and Jack decided to try out Blondy's suggestion on the truck but Jack had a spot of bother with a blowlamp and received some nasty burns necessitating use of our First Aid Box. Soon after 16:00 we moved on our way and the faulty truck ran quite well.

Making better progress, we passed Mareth and then through Medinien but soon came across the armoured car stopped just off the road with a blown tyre. This was the second blowout they had experienced on the journey and this time they had no spare wheel to use. We promised that if there was one available when we caught up with the Regiment at that night's leaguer, we would send it back to them.

So we passed on our way but within a few miles came up to another of our Squadron's lorries with some sort of engine trouble. Time was getting on so we straightaway took this vehicle in tow, hoping to catch up with the Regiment before dark. This we did not do, however, because last light came before passing Ben Gardane and there was still no sign of our leaguered Regiment. Continuing to crawl along, we eventually crossed the border into Tripolitania and, happily, our objective was eventually reached around 23:00. After a meal, Frank was able to obtain a spare wheel to suit the 'Flying Fitters' and, in a borrowed Jeep, set off back to the Medinien area where we had last seen them.

Our party had little sleep that night as early next morning saw the truck we towed in being made serviceable. The convoy moved off around 07:00 but soon we were left miles behind due to another blown tyre on our store lorry. This happened near Zuara about mid-morning and, of course, we had no serviceable spare this time so we pulled off the road hoping that LAD, now some way behind, might be able to help out.

The LAD had not leaguered with us overnight but it was known they had already parted with many tyres to many vehicles in need. While waiting we had a brew-up and I filled in some time washing out some 'smalls'. It is interesting to record that all along this important roadway there were many signs such as 'If you must brew-up, get off the road', or another 'Do not stop on the road – keep moving' and numerous others. I expect these were erected when supplies were being rushed up from Tripoli to the advancing 8th Army in Tunisia.

Our unwanted stop on this roadside lasted just four hours before the first LAD came along. This happened to be one of their heavy breakdown lorries and it had a vehicle of our type on suspended tow, so we were lucky to be able to exchange one of our unserviceable wheels for one of the suspended vehicle's front ones.

Our wheel change completed we set off at a good pace, for that part of the coastal road from the Tunisian border to Tripoli was excellent. We had come up this way in March so this time we passed through the little places of note in reverse order – Zuara (already mentioned), Sabratha, Suani, and Zavia. Before reaching Tripoli we branched off to the right and travelled mostly by track south of the city to a place called Azzizia, this being about 20 miles inland. This was not very far away from Saunnu where one night was spent on our way up to Tunisia. We reached the Regiment's leaguer rather late and at last light.

Next morning we were able to see the surroundings of our new home. Yes, it looked a fair spot, a large Italian-style farm settlement with some grass and some sandy areas but also with a number of small trees. Here a Regimental workshop was created by all the Squadron's fitters, motor mechanics and technical store lorries, linking with the LAD. Each day a few vehicles, both wheeled and track, were brought in for checking over or overhaul where required and for checking of tools and equipment. Thus, our party had little to do with C Squadron except for meals and mail. We were quite close to our Squadron though, just the other side of a railway track which ran through the area. It was strange to see trains pass along, usually three or four a day.

Our Squadron group increased numerically with several patrol size tents together in a row. Blondy, Bud, Jim and Bill shared one; Frank, Charlie and Jack shared another; George Bull was in with the rest of the motor mechanics, namely Nix Graham, Jock Spiers and Ken Barker. I stuck to my bivvy on the end of the row. Every evening we were here, however, there was a brew-up supper party in Charlie's tent to hear the wireless news from London and a chat on the latest news tips. It should be mentioned that, after a few days, Jack went in 'dock' with those burns on his hand received on the way up. Of the newcomers to our group, Nix hailed from Sussex, Ken from Derby and Jock from Airdrie in Scotland. Jock, like George, was about 6ft 2ins tall.

High Summer – Relaxing near Tripoli

Until 23 June 1943 we remained at Azzizia and it was exceedingly hot all the time, with temperatures reaching 120°F in the shade. Because of this, our work period was only 08:00 until noon and after lunch one had the choice of a siesta or of catching a truck to Tripoli for the afternoon and evening or just a brief trip for a swim. My days became a mixture of doing the above but my letter writing was done in the bivvy between 22:00 and midnight when it was a little cooler.

One day, which was somewhat different, was 7 June when, in the morning, I returned some unserviceable stores to an Ordnance Department in Tripoli. I came back to a late lunch and siesta and had a surprise when cookhouse served out ice-cold drinks mid-afternoon. This was something new but very acceptable in the heat. Alex came over to the bivvy for a chat in the evening.

The Regiment had a visit from General Montgomery on 15 June after which it was rumoured that we were going to have to move to the coast somewhere because of the intense heat. Also, soon after his visit, a notice went up regarding the coming visit to the area of General Lyon. There was speculation as to who was this General Lyon but what was true was that most personnel, if not all, were given 19 and 20 June off duties to spit and polish their best uniforms, etc. At 08:30 on 21 June the 10th Royal Hussars, in company with thousands of other troops, lined a route into Tripoli for the visit of HM the King.

Much other speculation went on while in this area. It was thought that most of our old vehicles would have to be handed in because of their poor condition and we wondered if we would have to go back to the Delta for new vehicles and equipment before perhaps going elsewhere.

The morning of 23 June found us employed in moving from Azzizia down to the coast. This was a move of roughly 30 miles but it took several hours to accomplish in convoy. We took the track previously travelled which by-passed the coastal city and our newest home was made right adjoining the sea at a spot near kilometre stone 29 on the coastal road Tripoli-Zuwarah. The Regimental workshop continued here so our first day was spent erecting tents and stripping everything from our store lorry, putting the bins and stores in a tent.

The Regiment was on rather a narrow strip of land so was spread out all along the shoreline with C Squadron being furthest away from the workshop this time, about a mile. Hence all personnel manning the workshop, except LAD, were attached to HQ Squadron for meals. Our party's tents were the same as before so I still had the bivvy for myself with a slit trench to make for headroom and greater comfort. I had now, as with most of our party, acquired a roughly made camp bed.

The day or half-day trips into Tripoli continued. For swimming, one could not beat the rock cove pool that the Regiment very soon set up. There were even Galas held at the cove pool while we were there.

Some of the days spent there can be highlighted to give an overall picture. To start with, it was still very hot indeed. One day, when in Tripoli, it was 125°F in the shade. It was ordered that we should drink 5 pints of water per day but all our water came out of metal containers and these, of course, got hot even when kept under vehicles for shade. We solved having to drink hot or warm water by standing the containers in the sea for a time.

26 June was spent doing a bit of work in the morning and bathing and sunbathing at the pool in the afternoon – most of the troops had by now purchased, or otherwise come by, a pair of swimming trunks. During the evening a mobile cinema unit paid a visit and so an open-air seashore crowd saw the picture "Much Too Shy" featuring George Formby.

On 27 June, a Sunday, a voluntary church service was held in the morning so George and I went along. We both enjoyed the open-air service conducted by a Brigade Chaplain. It was a rare thing to have such an event. The afternoon was spent at the cove pool and the weather made it 'just the job'. During the evening I spent some time with 'Taffy' Waite and friends of LAD who had a gramophone and records loaned to them from a Tripoli Club.

Most of 28 June I spent in HQ Technical Office, since most of their staff were away for one reason or another. Evening was spent at the canteen where the Regiment had erected a small marquee tent, but choices available were limited. However, a cup of tea or lemonade together with a chat was always welcome.

Next day, 29 June, George and I drew some food rations and obtained extra petrol because we were off on a two-day trip. All tanks left with the Regiment after the Tunisian campaign, numbering about 24, were to travel to Homs on transporters. There they were to be handed over to the 7th Armoured Division and I was sent for the purpose of the handing over. A further truck came too since the two-dozen tank drivers would need to be brought back. We left the area quite early using the route by-passing Tripoli. The transporters with the Sherman tanks travelled slowly and steadily, so our two trucks were able to have extra brew-up stops and then catch them up.

Homs, 70 miles east of Tripoli on the coast road, was reached at about 16:30 hours. The business of handing over was complete by 18:45. George and I had a look around Homs, not a big place, and went to see four one-act plays at a small theatre. The others went to a club for a drink. Later that evening we moved our lorry from the lorry park to join the tank drivers and other trucks on the beach to spend the night there. Next day, 30 June, we all enjoyed a breakfast of sausages and eggs with a swim afterwards before leaving at 10:30. The party reached the Tripoli bathing beach about 14:30 and partook of more bathing before finally reaching our Camp in time for the evening dinner.

On the first day of July I heard that all our transport was going to be handed over and in the course of the next few days this was done, except for the Technical Store lorries, cooks' lorries and other Quartermaster trucks and just a few of the newest lorries. Of these vehicles, I was concerned only with the handing over of our few scout cars and this was done near Castel Benito, not far away.

In the early days of July, I did several pleasure trips into Tripoli with Len Goring, who was in Technical HQ

Office and with whom I had left Bovington. We would normally have the afternoon at the Tripoli bathing beach and, after a meal at one of the numerous servicemen's clubs, go to a show. There were three main theatres in which 'buckshee' shows were put on. At the Union Club Theatre Len and I saw Ralph Reader's 'Gang Show', a relaxing evening of songs and comedy. It ran for a couple of weeks and so the main songs were often sung or whistled by the troops. Two favourites were "We'll all come home again some happy day" and "We're riding along on the crest of a wave".

Also early in July, Alex returned to the Regiment after several weeks away on some special duty. Also back was Jack – his burns now completely healed. One evening the mobile cinema came again, this time to give a special showing before a packed open-air audience of the film "Desert Victory".

There was a News Flash over the wireless on the morning of 10 July giving details of the invasion of Sicily, so that made it a day of note. The following day there was much interest in all news bulletins over the air. Charlie's little set was doing us fine and in the evening we had a full gathering for the supper brew-up and news.

25 July we heard that a move was imminent and that, surprisingly, it would be to the west and not east as most people thought likely. During the evening Alex sought me out and found me in the canteen. He had some news to give me. He was to act forthwith as Batman to an officer (Lt Johnstone) and in the morning he would be accompanying this officer to Palestine. The officer was going on a course there.

Next morning Nix Graham and I, of our group, joined with others going into Tripoli as volunteer blood donors. This did not take long so, after lunch, we saw an American stage show at the Miramar Theatre. After this we spent a couple of hours seated on the promenade watching the many ships in the harbour and bay. These included a number of troop ships, destroyers, cruisers and also a large hospital ship. There were others further out in the bay too. Some of the ships were flying barrage balloons and there were a number of these flying from the harbour itself. Tripoli seemed to be quite modern with most of its buildings glittering in the sun. Many of these buildings were of white concrete, including high apartment blocks and shops. Like most towns in this part of the world, it had its Arab quarters.

As if not to let us depart without a farewell, we had a sandstorm blow up on the evening of 27 July. It lasted most of the night too so in the morning a thick layer of sand covered everything in our tents. It was bathing before breakfast to rid our persons of the sand.

Our very last day in this area of North Africa came on 31 July. Our group was busy restoring our store lorry with its store bins, its stores and loads of extra kit. During the afternoon most had a farewell swim in our little cove and all were loath to leave. During the day many 1st Army Service Corps lorries arrived. They were to transport the 10th Royal Hussars as we were largely without transport of our own.

At the last minute about 80 men from the Regiment, mostly wheeled vehicle drivers, were detailed off to travel by ship to Alexandria and so on to Cairo. Their undertaking would be to ferry vehicles in convoy from the Middle East base at the Delta up to a North African base near Algiers. The party included some 25 from C Squadron including Jim, Nix and Ken from our recent workshop group.

CHAPTER TWELVE

WEST TO TUNISIA AGAIN

August to September 1943

The Cairo-bound party was left behind when, on Sunday 1 August, the Regimental convoy pulled out of our old spot on the coast near Tripoli at 06:45. As reported earlier, the coast road from Tripoli to the Tunisian border was an excellent one and so we were soon moving at a fair speed. There were more of us than usual travelling in our old technical store lorry but we mainly took up our customary positions. Blondy, Bud and George were in the cab, with Charlie, Frank and me up between the cab and body. Inside the truck were Jack and Jock. Eventually we passed through Sabratha with its imposing white church standing back off to the left of the road and then we travelled onwards towards Zuwarah. There were a number of date palm plantations along this stretch. As we neared Zuwarah, the road ran close to the sea and in the tiny bay were a couple of small Naval craft.

On crossing the border from Libya into Tunisia the road became a mere track which slowed the convoy to a crawl and everywhere, once again, was sand. It was like this for some 25 kilometres until the scrubby Arab town of Ben Gardane was reached. Four kilometres beyond this small town we leaguered up for the night.

On 2 August, breakfast was at 06:00 and we of our party remembered it was a Bank Holiday Monday in Blighty and we talked of where these holidays were often spent and of where we would like to spend the day. Such thoughts were in our minds all day but the weather back home was not always as great as here.

However, our journey recommenced at 07:00 and thoughts of the previous March came to mind as we passed Medinien and Mareth. At Mareth the first range of hills slowed us down and soon after, on reaching the top, a burst tyre brought our vehicle to a stop. We could hardly have stopped at a better spot for on one side of the road we helped ourselves to grapes from a huge vineyard and on the other side we picked a few pomegranates. This, and putting on our spare wheel, did not take long and we caught up with the convoy where they had halted for lunch. Once rolling again it was not long before Gabes was reached. The town was by-passed by a palm lined road, there being large bunches of unripe dates hanging from the palms.

Six kilometres beyond Gabes we leaguered up. Being only 15:00 hours it was announced that a number of lorries would be made available for anyone who wished to go into Gabes for swimming. Most of our party went and although the sea was very rough with big breakers rolling in we enjoyed jumping the waves. So you see, as it turned out, we did spend a couple of hours at the seaside on this August Bank Holiday Monday!

The next day, 3 August, was rather uneventful. On nearing the crossroad to Kuiranan we wondered if we would go that way since that was the way we travelled down in May. This time though, the convoy kept to the coast road and so into Sfax. Sfax we discovered to be quite a large town and port. Over the harbour area a good dozen barrage balloons floated in the air, shining like silver in the strong sunlight. There was no stop made, so we passed through on our way westwards. Leaguering spot that day was some 21 kilometres beyond Sfax and night-time saw us sleeping under the stars. At this point the 1st Army Service Corps lorries left the Regiment and the main portion of our troops continued the journey by train. Our party continued by road, the convoy now being only a small one.

4 August saw us on our way, still keeping to the coast road. The travelling became more and more pleasant as the sandy desert-like land gave way to groves of various types – vineyards and cultivation. We passed a very tiny town called El' Djem where, in a railway siding, we spotted our train party. There were loud cheers from both sides. Here too, just off the main roadway was a well-preserved and very sizeable Roman amphitheatre. Later we discovered that it was the oldest of its kind in North Africa. It was quite a surprise to find such a place miles from any large town.

The overnight stop came near Enfidaville at about 17: 00 hours. After dinner a few of our party roamed the groves picking grapes and figs. They also picked some prickly pears that are the fruit of the cactus, which seemed to be used for the purpose of hedging. The thick prickle-studded leaves were shaped like table-tennis bats and the fruits grew round the edges of these leaves. The fruit was very sweet and tasted of pear but the needle-like prickles could be very troublesome, as we found out. Enfidaville was a nice French-style village in rather a pleasant setting amid tall palms, vineyards and flowering shrubs.

An early start next day and we were soon going through Crombolia, the small town standing at the head of Cape Bon. It seemed mostly to be inhabited by Arabs, for the narrow streets were thronging with them. Very soon afterwards, we were passing a place known only too well by us – Sollum.

Shortly we saw the white buildings of Tunis shimmering in the heat-haze against the deep blue sea. Approaching the suburbs it was noticed how much the city had come alive again; busy rail sidings, factory sites and traffic reduced to a crawl. We came to the tramlines and saw that the tramcars were now operating. Our convoy vehicles became lost in traffic but the Military Police on traffic control were able to give us the route.

Some few kilometres beyond Tunis we saw the convoy halted, presumably to allow all the vehicles to come together. Now, we wondered, "where do we go from here?" Did I ever say that we had a little tune and words from the Western Desert, "Where do we go from here, now that we've passed Bordia ...?". Anyway, we took the Medjez El' Bab road which ran undulating across country. We discovered the town was only very small and had been knocked about a lot. Here we saw painted on a wall the American slogan "Praise the Lord and pass the ammunition". Underneath this, written in white, most likely by British troops, was, "Praise the Lord and pass the fly-swat". We tried to pick out the place – somewhere south of Medjez – where we were in May.

Later that afternoon we came to Berja, a larger town right in the centre of which we passed an enclosed football ground. After leaving Berja the country became quite mountainous. It was as much as the Hanamac with the office caravan trailer could manage on some hills. Yes, the Squadron had managed to retain those items of transport and usefulness.

Prison Guard Duties – D'Jebel Hallouf

We reached a place called Souk El' Khemis and turned off right up a minor road where, in about ten kilometres, we reached a mountain village and this proved to be our destination. There was a Regiment of troops at the village preparing to move out and we had to wait a time for this, after which we were to take over their duties. The main railway ran through Souk El' Khemis and our train party arrived within 20 hours of us. They had travelled up in rail trucks and not, as one might think, by comfortable rail coaches. The track of this railway up from Tunis was the same standard gauge as those at home. During our stay in the area we saw many huge American engines pulling long lines of trucks. Indeed, I think the Yanks were actually running this railway at the time.

The time for moving into the village came, tents were erected and soon everything was shipshape. The name of this village, which was to be our new home for a time, was D'Jebel Hallouf. We learnt that our sole duty here would be to provide guards at the very large Prisoner of War Camp at Souk El' Khemis. Infantry Regiments usually performed such duties but on this occasion we had to undertake the job for a time. As a sizeable part of the Regiment was away at the Delta the duties fell rather heavily on us. There were a large number required on the 24-hour guard at the POW Camp together with a normal night-guard in our own area of D'Jebel Hallouf.

At first, all of our party took part in these duties since there was little or no normal work to do. Sometimes there were even more personnel of the Regiment away because guards also had to be provided to escort parties of prisoners being transferred elsewhere. Frank, George and Jack went on such a trip into Algeria.

After a couple of weeks, an arms store was created that took the form of a fair-sized tent situated between two palm trees. I was put in charge of it, so was then gladly relieved of all other guard duties but had also to sleep there so had to move my bed. A tank trooper by the name of Jock McLeod was put with me as a mate. All the Squadron's small arms were kept there, both rifles and pistols, except those out with the guards at any given time. For me, this time at D'Jebel Hallouf became very comfortable but I was more or less tied to the store all the time.

D'Jebel Hallouf was only a small village but there were some lovely houses and villas and it was in a pleasant setting. There were numerous palm and conifer trees and some splendid views all around, especially looking down across the plain towards where Souk El' Khemis lay nestling in the hot and hazy sun. The centre of the village was a small open square and on one side was a little RC Church where, outside, were hung three bars of rusty iron used as bells. On another side stood the village hall which, with gallery, could seat about 150 people. It also had a small stage and facilities for show-ing films. This hall was used as a Squadron canteen but, apart from tea and wads[1], its items for sale were lim-ited to essentials like cigarettes, matches, razor blades and soap. It is worth mentioning that our money had changed several times since landing with English cur-rency in our pockets in Egypt in 1941. First came the coinage of Egypt, the Piastre, and then in Tripolitania we used the special British Military paper money and in Tunisia the paper Francs.

At D'Jebel Hallouf there was the occasional picture show in the village hall and sometimes too the Prisoner of War Camp Band presented a concert. This band of musicians was all Italian, with the exception of one lone German, and a couple of them had good voices too. Once or twice transport was made available for special shows in Tunis such as personal appearances of Gracie Fields or George Formby but I did not attend any of these.

The end of the first week in September saw the large contingent of Regimental troops who had been away turn up at D'Jebel Hallouf. They had finished ferrying the wheeled vehicles (loaded with all kinds of stores) to a base in Algeria and had all enjoyed a four-day leave in Cairo. Alex Watts also returned from Palestine, to-gether with the officer, and had taken seven days' leave at Cairo on the way back. About 20 September George Bull, not feeling too good, decided to go on sick parade. He returned with the news that he was to go in 'dock' and later we heard that he had malaria.

The weather was very hot indeed and flies were a constant irritation. One day it was announced on the Squadron Order Board that a prize of 100 cigarettes would be given to the tent which caught the most flies in one week, dead or alive. Each tent already had a fly catching system installed. It consisted of a glass jar, probably a jam jar, with a small hole and bait of sweet jam. The flies could get in but not out of this contraption. The winning tent reckoned they tallied up a thousand bodies. If that was from one tent then there must have been many, many flies 'down for the count'.

We had for some time been subject to anti-malaria measures. Here at D'Jebel Hallouf daily orders required "08:30 hours Mugs on Parade". Yes, it really meant mugs and not just us, and the mugs had to contain some water. This was for the purpose of washing down the Mepacream Tablets issued out and which had to be taken on parade. The measures were also strict with regard to our sleeping under mosquito nets, which had been part of our equipment for quite a while but not always used.

During this time of September a very strong rumour was prevalent that our Brigade was soon to return to the UK. So strong was this rumour that it included all ranks and everyone seemed of good spirit. A number of things occurred which seemed to give weight to the rumour, such as a strict check of every man's kit, the checking of leave obtained over the past nine months and also enquiries about whether anyone had a kit bag in any other store apart from the Regimental store in Alexandria (our kit bags with unwanted kit went to this store when we landed in Egypt.) Our Sergeant's tent started off a catchphrase which became very popular. One was quite often greeted with – "Have you seen the writing on the wall?" referring, of course, to the orders which seemed to uphold the rumour. We all had dreams of Blighty at this time.

One evening there was a 1st Army Group Concert Party giving a show at the village hall and the whole show was hilarious. The highlight of the concert party was an act by two clowns who, with faces and hands whitened, were named 'Malaria' and 'Dysentery'.

During September I was persuaded to take an exam that would give me Technical Storeman Class II status. This involved about a one hour written exam, plus an on-sight identification of spare parts. A few days later I heard the result was a pass.

On 29 September a Regiment of the Dorsets arrived at D'Jebel Hallouf to take over our duties. They arrived with battle dress and very pale faces and we soon learnt they were less than three weeks out from England. These men were a special Regiment of the Dorsets for they were all over 40 years of age and had volunteered as occupational troops in North Africa. On the evening of the 30th they gave a thank-you concert for 10th Royal Hussars in the village hall with a small band, etc. Near the end, the officers of both Regiments exchanged good wishes, the CO of the Dorsets saying his Regiment were honoured to be taking over the duties of a Regiment of the 8th Army and would follow their further exploits with interest. Community singing ended the evening and the roof was raised when their band struck up "Take me back to dear old Blighty".

Footnotes

[1] Wad – Type of rock cake or sandwich

CHAPTER THIRTEEN

ACROSS THE ATLAS MOUNTAINS
October 1943

1 and 2 October were busy days packing up. We had now heard that we would be moving west to Algeria and, in fact, to the Algiers area. Most of the Regiment would be travelling by train as at this time we had very little transport. The C Squadron technical store lorry and several others had been handed over since arrival at D'Jebel Hallouf. I was told that the B Squadron technical store lorry would accommodate both me and my stores and spares. Thus my store bins (four metal ones) with odds and ends and my own personal equipment were duly loaded on to their old six-wheeled Albion truck. A number of RASC vehicles arrived at D'Jebel Hallouf to run loads of kit and equipment down to Souk El' Khemis for transfer by train.

3 October saw all tents down by 09:30 hours and these were the last items of equipment to be transferred to train. A general clear up of the area followed and at 16:00 the train party departed, being played out of the village by the Dorset Regiment's band. The road party, which consisted of about 60 of us, slept that night in the village hall.

Our reveille the next morning, 4 October, was at 04:00 hours. After a cup of tea and a wash and shave we were ready for a 05:00 move. My mates for this trip were Corporal 'Dolly' Dalton who was B Squadron technical storeman, Sergeant Harry Sandy and Trooper Jacky

Slater, both of that Squadron's fitters. A new procedure was to give each vehicle a route card of towns and places to be passed through and we knew the journey was to be over 500 kilometres. As daylight drifted in so this little convoy drifted out of D'Jebel Hallouf. Our C Squadron water truck and the Hanamac pulling the caravan office were just to the rear of us.

It did not take us long to reach Souk El' Khemis where we saw the train party all out washing and shaving, so they must have spent the night in the trucks on the railway sidings. 'Dolly' and I were seated high up between the body and cab of this old Albion truck and the early morning air was quite nippy.

A good run of level roadway took us, in about 15 kilometres, to Souk El' Arab, the road running over an unusual number of long bridges. Some of these were bridges over rivers and some were over wadis but they were of the same pattern. There were two cooks' lorries in the convoy and a stop for breakfast came soon after passing this town.

Not long after being on the move again it became obvious we would soon start climbing, since nothing but mountains lay ahead. These were the Atlas Mountains. Sure enough, we saw where the railway disappeared into a tunnel and then we struck the bottom of the pass. We twisted and turned in almost every direction around horseshoe bends as we climbed the pass. At this point the mountains were very bleak. Even after reaching the top of the first pass we discovered the road to be a proper up and down affair.

Whilst moving on one of the 'ups', our vehicle engine spluttered and came to a stop. It seemed to be a fuel stoppage so, while the two fitters started dismantling the carburettor and fuel pump, 'Dolly' and I were seeing to a brew-up. It was fully a couple of hours before the engine was running to the satisfaction of the fitters but we had a further brew-up before moving off. Any hope of catching the convoy that night was almost nil.

The scenery began to change to deep wooded valleys and presently we began to drop downhill in a series of wide sweeping bends round the hills. On rounding one such bend we saw the railway track in the valley. It wound along this valley to where, in the distance, was a town. We soon found ourselves on a road running parallel to the rails and so reached the small town of Souk El' Arris. We halted in the town at a canteen for a tea and wad and here decided to pull a short way out of the town and leaguer up for the night.

It was a stiff climb out of town before we came to an ideal piece of open land on one side of the road. Here, half a dozen vehicles were apparently leaguered for the night, so we pulled in alongside them. It turned out they were the advance party of some of our Divisional Royal Corps of Signals. This was where I discovered the loss of my bedding roll and on telling the 'signal' boys about it they said they too had lost a bedding roll and haversack. Between us we came to the conclusion that, while rounding some of those steep mountain bends, Arabs must have climbed aboard. We remembered passing little groups of Arabs on those mountain roads. No good crying over 'spilt milk' as it were, so we soon settled for the night, my three buddies each loaning me a blanket.

Being on our own like this we were able to lie-in until the sun was well up. Thus, by the time we had purchased eggs from Arabs who had gathered round and had our breakfast it was nearly 09:45 hours. Once on our way this day, 5 October, we soon came to a small village and a nearby DID centre. Here we stopped while Sergeant Sandy went in to try to obtain some food rations for us. He was lucky and called for help to carry a wooden box loaded with rations of all kinds. Later on we passed one of the few places along that stretch of road, namely Lavadore, a French-style village of some beauty, hidden away in the mountains.

At about 16:00 we came to a small Arab township and on the far side was a Traffic Control Post. The Military Police on duty were able to tell us that the 10th Royal Hussars convoy had passed through at 13:00 hours and was hoping to reach the next staging area some 75 kilometres further on in order to spend the night. As it was then late afternoon, he advised us to pull in at this staging area because there was nowhere to leaguer for the night in between the two stages. We took his advice and so had an early night after a smashing meal of bacon, eggs, fried tomatoes and bread.

The following morning thunder and lightning accompanied pouring rain. We were sleeping under the stars and soon made a quick dash into the lorry where we sat in dozy fashion, with a blanket or two draped about us, for a couple of hours. Thus we managed to be on the move somewhat more promptly on 6 October. The scenery throughout the day's run was really great, similar to North Wales. Places we passed were Duvivier, Tilergma, Oued, Sitif, and Beni

Manover. It rained during the latter part of the day and the muddy, slippery road was none too safe in places as we travelled over the mountains.

In order to reach a staging area we were forced into travelling after dark but fortunately not for long because we came across some Nissan huts by the road with windows ablaze with light. After inquiring, we pulled in and so slept that night in a hut with a nice cosy fire. This was 'just the job' after some hours of rain.

On 7 October we managed to hit the trail by 10:00 and about 500 yards up the road, still in the staging area, we pulled into a petrol point to fill up our tank and the reserve tins, which had been used up. The Corporal on duty there enlightened us to the fact that the Regimental convoy had leaguered there that night but had pulled out at 07:00 that morning. So it seemed we had caught up with them but had been unaware of the fact – and they were away again while our little group was still tucked up in bed. However, we had our fill of petrol and got under way, passing more lovely country where every turn of the road brought us fresh views.

During the morning ride we went through two fair-sized towns, namely Douria and Palestro and also passed a big American convoy moving in the opposite direction. We pulled into a nice wooded spot for our lunch and, as usual, Arabs soon gathered around. Also, as usual, we bartered for some eggs and soon struck a bargain. I wonder? We seemed to be living on eggs for this trip and for lunch had three boiled ones each!

On continuing our journey we soon came to a thrilling section of landscape. The railway and road were following the course of a river and for several kilometres all three ran together through a narrow gorge. The river was at the lowest level whilst, raised up some 30 feet on either side, were the railway and roadway. Actually the Yanky term 'canyon' would better describe it I think. It was so narrow in places that the railway or road, or indeed both, ran through short tunnels. This stretch of road and rail was a wonderful feat of engineering as was much of the road during our four day's travel over the Atlas Mountains.

We were now passing towns and villages more frequently and we next passed through Meiverville, Alma and Fondouk. We were driving along the foothills of the mountains and to our right lay a great fertile plain. We came to this plain, passing Arba and Bouinan, before reaching Boufarik with daylight rapidly slipping away. We enquired of an MP where 10th Royal Hussars were leaguered. We knew the Regiment's new area was in the vicinity of Boufarik. Being directed along a by-road we shortly came to the 10th Royal Hussars' sign pointing up a narrow track. I soon discovered where C Squadron fitters and, in particular, our party had the patrol tent erected. Very soon I was settled in with them and had also reported the loss of my bedding roll. Charlie, Frank & Co fixed me up with bedding for the time being.

Each Army Regiment carried its sign on all vehicles, usually two at the front and two at the rear. Our Brigade was known by the rhinoceros in white on black background and our Regiment by a red 67 on a white background. We were, therefore, sometimes referred to as 'The Rhinos'.

CHAPTER FOURTEEN

ST MARGUERITE

October to December 1943

It took only a few days for the situation of our new area to impress us. The country all about was most fertile with acres of vineyards, orange, lemon and fig groves. The French people of the village always seemed to be busy with their jobs, while Arab boys tended to the herds of cows and ploughed and moved goods around locally with teams of four or six oxen. In the far distance, yet seeming to rise high above us, were the heights and peaks of the mountains. These mountains, like those we had recently travelled, were part of the Atlas range.

Here at St Marguerite dwelt A, B & C Squadrons, whilst HQ was stationed at a smaller farm some ¾ mile away. A Squadron office, SQM stores, technical stores and fitters, etc, could be found among the big Dutch barns and farmyards. The main body of troops, however, was billeted on the top floor of a wine press and they were in rather cramped conditions. Other buildings still retained by the village people included a carpenter's shop, a wheelwright's and an engineering shop where farm implements were doctored. There were also a blacksmith's and a basket-making shop. In this area was a very big barn, fully enclosed and probably used for the storage of farm produce and equipment.

My storage bins and other items of stores were off-loaded from the B Squadron technical store lorry and placed along the back wall of our party's patrol tent. Charlie had the wireless working so we were quickly settled in and feeling homely.

We soon discovered that the Regiment had brought along the Prisoner of War Camp Band from the D'Jebel Hallouf area. The party of about 20 Italians and one solitary German was versatile and talented. The German, a slightly built young man, played the accordion. An outbuilding near the wine press was turned into a canteen and the band would entertain here about three evenings a week. They also entertained in both the officers' and Sergeants' areas. These prisoners were given plenty of rope, being allowed to eat and mix with us. Indeed one or two were talented cooks and almost took over the cookhouse whilst others did various jobs about the area.

Of course, we soon got to know quite a lot about these men and some became popular characters. The leader of the outfit we discovered to be a Professor of Music and he was a wonderful player of the flute and piccolo. He wrote some of the music the band played and he composed one tune called the 10th Hussars. The German, too, became popular. He used to come over to our tent and have long conversations with Frank and he could speak English, French and Italian.

On 10 October I was instructed to go over to an Ordnance Depot near Boufarik taking three drivers in order to pick up three tanks. It was understood these would be for training purposes only but they were, nevertheless, brand new Sherman tanks. These became the first tanks our Squadron had possessed for about three months and this was so with the other Squadrons, who had likewise drawn a few each.

On the morning of the 15 October I was ordered to attend a Court of Inquiry regarding the loss of my bedding roll. The loss was not just groundsheet and blankets, for rolled up inside these were a pair of KD slacks, a pair of KD shorts, one KD shirt, a pair of plimsolls and a mosquito net. The Court was held at our Squadron Office and consisted of three officers. Captain Lloyd of C Squadron acted as Chairman while the others were Lieutenants from A and B Squadrons. Those who travelled on the same vehicle were in attendance too and we were called in one at a time, me being the first. The statements were taken on Oath. On being marched into the office I gave a smart salute after which one of the Lieutenants said, "Put your hand on the Bible and repeat what I say". Well, unfortunately, this officer stuttered a bit and so what I should have said would be something like this: "I...I... sw...swear b...by by Al...Almighty Go...Go...God", and so on. I think I had finished way ahead of him! However, it was all a new experience for me and fortunately the Court must have ruled in my favour as I was instructed to draw new kit to replace all that was lost.

Monday 18 October brought a very rare event, this being none other than a kit inspection. All items of our personal kit were laid out spick and span. This was all to do with a forthcoming Brigadier's visit, parade and inspection.

By 20 October one or two of the few lorries we had were made available for troops to spend a day in Algiers and Alex and I decided to go one day. We roamed around together seeing the sights and people. It gave us a unique feeling of freedom to be amongst people in a city once again, even though these very people were hurrying about their business and took no notice of us. Of course, there were lots of uniformed people about as well and it made a change to see a few Naval 'boys'. We went to a cinema during the afternoon and saw an English talkie featuring Judy Garland. Often we heard her sing on the wireless in 'Forces Favourites'. Not liking the French food dishes, we used one or other of the numerous service clubs for our meals but were only able to obtain tea, tomato sandwiches and little fancy cakes.

The city buildings were quite modern, most of them having very large windows and sun verandas. The Postal and Telegraph building in Rue de Islet was one of the most impressive. Tramcars or trolley buses ran through all the main streets. The city was a pleasant one, built on the steep slopes of a hill that ran down to the sea, with all the main streets terraced across the slope parallel to the sea.

Along by the sea and docks ran the railway whilst the promenade was some 20 feet above. The next main road up appeared to run along the rooftops of buildings on the promenade facing the sea. For this reason a number of these main streets had buildings only on the landward side, the other being open to streets below and the sea. In many cases flights of steps were the link from one main street to another. There was, of course, an older part of Algiers and this was largely the Arab section with its Casbah and Bazaar.

About this time some bits and pieces of timber were finding their way into our Camp area and those of us who camped outside the main billets began making beds for ourselves. The 'Flying Fitters' who camped next door to us were the first to do this and so it caught on. There was no pattern, plan or design laid down. The timber, mostly 3in by 2in, had to form a rectangle roughly 6ft by 2½ft and then have four legs attached. It was a laugh to see the various types our party knocked up. Jack's especially was a masterpiece of 'Heath Robinson' design and not one of us was surprised that it let him down (not lightly) the first night of use! Jock's bed was made with very long legs – he must have taken the pattern from his own legs because he stood 6ft 1in – and it looked like a table. My bed had short thick legs and was very solid. I once boasted of it being most stable and was immediately reminded that animals slept in a stable!

Around this period of time came the first fruits from the orange groves and we turned our carpentry skills into fashioning boxes of all kinds suitable for sending some fruit home. Here we were surrounded by so many orange groves whereas at home fruit was almost unobtainable. We later learnt that a certain centre in Algiers would accept orders for sending boxes of various fruits home so many of us took advantage of this service.

Now that we had been in the area of St Marguerite a few weeks some of the French villagers were becoming friendly. One elderly Frenchman, a short dapper chap who always wore a black beret on his head, began to call for any dirty linen to be washed. He lived in one of a few cottages grouped together on the Boufarik road. Jack took control of this business and so the 'old boy' came to always ask for Monsieur Jacko. Now Jack knew about two words in French one of which was, luckily,

"Compri". You can imagine the wonderful conversation between the 'old boy' and Jack. Oftentimes we were in fits of laughter and, of course, Jack was egged on by us. Jack would speak in an ordinary tone of voice, always finishing up with "Compri?"; the 'old boy' would say, "Non compri", whereupon Jack would shout as if talking to a deaf man and, at every "Non compri", Jack's voice would rise to a higher pitch. It usually ended with a kind of charade, with Jack doing the acting to make the 'old boy' understand. This became a twice-weekly pantomime over the long period we remained there.

On Sunday 24 October another unusual event was held. This was an 'All Hands' Church Parade held in the morning at the big barn. It was held to commemorate the anniversary of El' Alamein and was quite a nice event – one which brought back the happenings of the previous year. The barn really was huge, being entirely enclosed and having a glass roof. About one third of the barn's floor area at one end was made available for the church service. I don't know where all the seating came from but it comprised mostly wooden forms. Later on a decent stage was erected and all kinds of events took place there, including picture shows and concerts.

Towards the end of October we were pleased to see the return of George Bull to the Regiment and to our Squadron. We listened sympathetically to his story since leaving us at D'Jebel Hallouf. He had gone into hospital with malaria and, having recovered from that, was eventually flown up to Algiers. Unfortunately George had to report sick again and so went into hospital again, this time with yellow jaundice. Now feeling very fit, he had to rejoin Transport Troop who were accommodated with most others at the wine press building.

At the beginning of November Charlie discovered that his brother Fred was stationed at Boufarik. He was soon able to contact him and our party were all introduced. His brother was part of the RAF ground staff and soon he and a pal made frequent visits to us. One afternoon all our party went over to his Station and were shown around the workshops and also shown a few kites on the airfield, which was very interesting.

Through correspondence I learnt that an old friend of mine, Norman Anderson, was stationed at Phillipville in Algeria. He wrote to me, "I have been up to Algiers a couple of times and looked about everywhere for your Regiment, without success".

During November we were made up to strength with regard to wheeled vehicles. One of the new vehicles was a 15cwt Bedford truck and this was often used as a runabout truck in the area. With permission, I quite often used it to run the mile or so to the HQ Technical Office. All the wheeled vehicles were kept on a piece of open ground near our camping area between two large Dutch barns. We were also gradually building up our quota of tanks and these were used at a nearby spot for practice of a new gunnery technique.

About the middle of November, George made the discovery that voluntary Free Church services were held for any service people of our Division on Sunday evenings at 18:30 at Boufarik Presbyterian Church. The following weekend we decided to go and so we walked the three and a half kilometres to the little church in the main square of Boufarik. That first Sunday we had to stand up at the back but extra chairs were brought in on the numerous other occasions when we went. Everything about these services was bright and cheerful with singing going with a swing. The Methodist Padre was a welcoming personality and his face had a beaming smile on it all the time. The troops used to take part sometimes either reading the Lesson or giving a solo.

The afternoon of 28 November saw our party on a trip up to Chrea which was reputed to be a French winter resort in the Atlas Mountains. The way led through Boufarik and a straight road of a dozen kilometres to Blida which was a large town lying at the edge of the plain with the mountains rising high beyond. The narrow road that wound its way up to Chrea was an amazing one. It started off with only a steady rise and not many bends. Before long we obtained a grand view of the expanse of the plain. The towns, miles apart, seemed to draw in close together and Blida, at the foot, reflected a dazzle of white in the sun against the green of the groves and reddish-brown of ploughed land. Soon, far in the distance, we could see where the deep blue Mediterranean Sea met the blue of the sky. The road became steeper as it zigzagged its way up wooded gorges until, at 5,600 feet, was a delightful village in a snowy setting.

The village was of wooden villas scattered among the pine trees. We threw snowballs and pine cones at each other just for fun as we walked towards a clearing in the trees. Here, in full swing, was a party indulging in the vigorous art of skiing. It was a very nice trip indeed and most pleasant to be able to breathe some cooler air for a change.

About this time Alex, who had been a batman to an officer for some months, returned as a transport driver. It happened this way: Our Squadron's batmen had a comfortable patrol tent near the officer's quarters but one evening while making a brew-up on a primus stove there was an accident. A bottle of petrol was knocked over and the fire that followed destroyed the tent, much of the batmen's kit and even some officers' kit. A wooden trunk had recently arrived from India and contained lots of personal items and kit belonging to Lieutenant Lord Ednam. Now this officer was returning from India to re-join his Regiment (10th Royal Hussars) but, as he had not yet arrived, the trunk was put in charge of the batmen. It and the contents were mostly lost in the fire. A Court of Inquiry was held but the only result as far as Alex knew was that the batmen were reduced to one between two officers. Alex did not mind returning to driving.

After much bargaining with an old Arab our party had bought a few chickens some time previously. These birds had been fattened up with scraps of food, Army biscuits and fresh air! Our party decided to have a feast on Sunday 12 December in the form of an early Christmas dinner. Jack was an all-rounder who claimed to have done a spot of 'fowl' business in Civvy Street. One of his best stories was the account of his purchase of a donkey and cart with numerous laughable incidents – but that was another tale. To a critical and leg-pulling audience Jack demonstrated the art of killing, plucking, trimming and tying the birds. He also gave a lecture on the 'inner workings of a fowl', withdrawing and placing the innards on the table as exhibits 1, 2, 3 and so on. The Italian helpers cooked those birds to perfection and our meal was a great success.

On 14 December an impromptu concert for the Regiment was held in the big barn, which had now been partitioned off with canvas. More canvas, which had been painted, had been used to seal off each side of the stage One depicted a life-size Christmas party in progress and the other was of a large liner churning through the sea and given the name 'Blighty'. Bunting and flags also helped to create a cheerful atmosphere.

During the Division's stay in this area, many shows of all kinds were held so that one could always go to some entertainment or other. The Service Corps had turned a wine factory located between Boufarik and Blida into quite a good theatre, seating up to 2,000 troops. Picture or stage shows were held regularly. Shows were also held at Boufarik, our own big barn and, of course, in Algiers.

During mid-December loads of timber were fetched from the docks at Algiers. This timber was part of the huge packing cases in which stores, engines and other large spare parts had been brought over for the war. It was understood that wooden buildings were to be erected in the place of tents, mainly because of the much talked about rainy season! In C Squadron there were just four groups housed in tents and we were close together between two massive Dutch barns. The Squadron Quartermaster Stores was the first hut we built, followed by a Gun Store. The 'Flying Fitters' and our party intended to wait until after Christmas to begin building.

CHAPTER FIFTEEN

STILL IN ST MARGUERITE

December 1943 to May 1944

Christmas

The 1943 Christmas was my best festive season since joining the Army. On Christmas Eve, soon after break-fast, someone of our party suggested going into Algiers for the day. So four of us obtained passes, (Jack, Jock, Nix and I) and as we had been a little late in making up our minds, we missed the Squadron's provided transport. However, we had no trouble in managing to hitchhike. Algiers was in a festive mood with shops and clubs gaily decorated and all and sundry in very cheerful spirit. We enjoyed an afternoon picture show and altogether had a really nice day, returning to Camp by the Squadron truck.

The St Marguerite Camp area was lively until a late hour. Some of our party rigged up a large stocking for Jack's benefit and filled it with all kinds of things – mostly his own! This created some fun on the Christmas morn-ing as Jack, sitting up in bed, insisted on going into every item of his big stocking. To the stocking we had attached a card stating "Merry Christmas to the Earl of Essex from friend Tom Sawyer". It was a running joke that Tom Sawyer was the maker of those soya & link sausages that were standard breakfast rations and which Jack did not enjoy.

Breakfast was fried bacon and two eggs. At 09:30 a voluntary church service was held in the big barn and there was a surprising number in attendance. Alex was there and so afterwards we went for a good long walk. I ought to mention now that the Regiment were acting as hosts over the Christmas period to 25 British sailors off a ship in Algiers harbour.

The Regiment's Christmas dinner was held in the big barn and before 13:00 hours everyone was seated while our Italian band provided music. In normal Army custom, officers served and waited on all other ranks for this splendid do. Our menu was roast chicken or turkey with cauliflower and roast and boiled potatoes, followed by Christmas pudding, custard and mince pies, dates and oranges. There was wine or beer and plenty of cigarettes. It really was a very enjoyable affair, so very different from our 1941 Christmas meal.

During the afternoon, a fancy dress polo match was held. It was 'Officers versus Sergeants'. This was played with hockey sticks and a football and the 'mounts' were very small and weak-looking donkeys. We laughed our heads off, such were the antics of both players and beasts. One officer, dressed only in bathing trunks and a dispatch rider's helmet with two large feathers, kept getting off his donkey and winding him up by the tail. Another, dressed in dinner outfit complete with frock tailcoat and top hat, was soon unrecognisable, so often was he pitched into the wet mud.

A late tea was held in the big barn and a Christmas party, to which the French locals were invited, followed this.

Boxing Day morning was wet so after breakfast at 09: 00 all our party returned to bed. Alex came over at 11: 30 so I got up and we went for a nice walk since the sun was then shining. That afternoon an American Concert Party gave a show at the big barn. This was quite a good show during which our guests, the sailors, were enticed on to the stage to sing a few sea shanties.

At 18:00 hours on Boxing Day, our party accepted an invitation to go to dinner at one of the French cottages. Our hosts were an elderly couple who, since our arrival, had been doing our washing (and doing it well) for a reasonable charge. Whilst Madame finished preparing, the 'old boy' showed pictures of their sons and daughters and so on. We enjoyed a four-course meal of soup, bread, mixed vegetables, followed by three roast chickens and then oranges and wine. At 20:00 we took the old couple back to the big barn where, to a packed audience of troops and civilians, the film Charlie's Aunt was shown. The picture caused many laughs and was just right for our happy mood.

With Christmas behind us both our party and the 'Flying Fitters' started the building of our respective wooden huts. These were both completed by the end of December so the start of a New Year saw us well and truly settled in.

Our party's shanty was about 24 feet by 14 feet and at each side of the doorway were square shutters that could be taken down during the day to provide open windows. We also made a fireplace suitable for wood fires. Frank, having become keen on photography, required a darkroom and so a partition was provided at the rear of the shanty with also some space for my metal store bins. Charlie's brother was able to supply Frank with film and printing paper and other equipment for doing enlargements, etc.

New Year

The first month of the New Year proved to be a busier time for our party and for me in particular. This was because the Squadron had become fully equipped with tanks and support vehicles. Up to Christmas we had only been partially equipped.

All the evening shows continued and each night a lorry or two would go from the Squadron packed with troops for the RASC theatre. Every Thursday and Saturday saw a half-day off with a full day off on Sundays. On these days, trips continued to be run into Algiers. Two members of the Italian band started up a barbers shop and they did a roaring trade (and enriched themselves as well).

About mid-January the news spread of a forthcoming Regimental exercise to take place somewhere in the mountains. We had a new 3-ton vehicle allocated as Technical Store Lorry and so this had to be fitted out with the store bins and other items. The 'Flying Fitters' also had a new armoured car, which this time was complete with wireless equipment.

About 20 January our Squadron held a big dance and social evening in Algiers. Nearly all our lorries were used to ferry in those wishing to go – and most of them did. However, I did not attend but remained to look after our little group of shanties. My beauty sleep was disturbed by the merriment of our party when they returned at about 02:30 hours.

The move up into the mountains came on 29 January. The tanks went most of the way by train but our support vehicles went in convoy by road, departing at 05:00 hours. The Italian band went on loan, so we were told, for a few weeks to another Regiment but it transpired we never ever saw them again.

The trip into the hills was enjoyable, the route being back along the same road as that of the last day of travel up from D'Jebel Hallouf. The destination was a high and exposed plateau above the town of Bouira behind which, like sentinels, stood several high mountain peaks, their upper halves bearing a mantle of snow.

For some days the sun shone in all its glory and the snow-covered peaks provided a grand picture especially when at sunset the snow took on a red hue. The evenings and nights, however, were very cold indeed. We were all under canvas with our party being in the patrol tent at the tank park. The 'Flying Fitters' were in their tent some five minutes' walk from the rest of the Squadron. We wished our fireplace at the shanty had been brought along. Permission was granted after a week of suffering cold nights for a certain type of fireplace to be fitted in the tents. In no time at all we had one fitted, thanks to Charlie and Frank who did the work. Fuel was at first a problem but the discovery that a certain Frenchman at Bouira might be persuaded to sell charcoal eased the situation. From then on a charcoal fire it was.

The tanks and echelons were on exercises most days but although the 'Flying Fitters' were involved, we never once moved. The plan was to stay in the hills for six weeks carrying out training exercises but, in the end, weather took a hand in the scheme of things. From the sky fell every form of moisture and soon a sea of mud was over the top of our boots. Heavy wire netting and coconut matting had to be laid in some places as a runway for the wheeled vehicles. My work entailed carrying out a daily on-foot inspection of vehicles of all types and sending a daily return of the state of vehicles to Technical HQ. An old pal, 'Taffy' Waite of LAD, did me a good turn once again by loaning me a pair of wellington boots.

Everything came to a complete stop when one night it blew a blizzard and snow fell very heavily. That night our tent collapsed under the weight of snow so at about 01:20 hours some of us were trying to hold the tent erect while others were out knocking in pegs and sorting out guy ropes. Only Jack of our party stayed in bed and when we chipped him about it he claimed, "I was trapped in my bed". Snow continued to fall that day and nothing moved then or for the next few days.

On 19 February orders came 'Exercise cancelled'. Tanks were to stay where they were with each driver remaining to form a guard for the vehicle park. Everyone else was to pack up right away and return to St Marguerite. It certainly was a treat returning to our shanty where there was no sign of snow. It was early March when the tanks came rolling back.

Easter 1944

The second week in March saw the Royal Tank Regimental Band come to stay in our area while giving concerts in the area. They stayed about two weeks and gave one show at the big barn, which was very good.

Also in March, football came on to the agenda when the Division started a knockout competition. Our Squadron was the only one interested in our Regiment so we entered for this. The first game was away somewhere versus another Regiment and resulted in a 5-1 win. I played in this game.

Most of that month and early April was much as normal, a mixed routine of work and leisure which together created a form of pleasure. George, I and sometimes one or two others, kept up the habit of attending the service on Sunday evenings at Boufarik. We enjoyed the habit of walking in and, after the service, going to the Salvation Army Club for tea and a bun before walking back.

Many of the evenings were spent at the shanty, though the cosy fire became less necessary. Often Alex would come over for a chat or sometimes we might go to a show, either at the big barn or the RASC theatre.

It was a change to accompany Len Goring into Algiers for the day on 25 March. The highlight of the day was the big football game we attended in the evening, which was the 8th Army versus the RAF. The Algiers stadium was well filled with servicemen in uniforms of all types. The pitch was completely bare of grass. It was an enjoyable game with the 8th Army winning 5-1. One young man who played for the 8th Army came from The Queen's Boys of our Brigade. Pre-war an English club had just taken him on. After the war he played regularly in the 1st Division and starred as a winger for both Preston North End and England. No prizes for guessing his name – Tom Finney.

In April sea bathing started with the nearest two places being Castlellion and Dooara Marine, both about 18 kilometres away. At each of these places there was a small town and the seafronts included short promenades.

7th April was Good Friday but none of our party left Camp. Instead we spent a quiet, restful day at the shanty. The next day, however, 'Nix' and I joined up to go into Algiers. We left about 11:00 and made our own way in by thumbing a lift. After a lunch at a services club, we went to the Empire 'Forces Free' Cinema and saw the film 'Northern Pursuit'. At 18:30 we were part of a big holiday crowd of service personnel and French civilians at the football stadium. The game was Combined Services v France, and the Services XI ran out easy winners by 7-3.

Easter Sunday was much the same as other Sundays of late with George and I having our usual 'date' in the evening. Easter Monday, 10 April, our party and a couple of the SQMS chaps went off around mid-morning taking our store lorry for the day. We went on the coast road to Sidi Faroush, where the beach was quiet and smashing for bathing. The beach was of very fine shingle, almost sand-like, and was backed by grassy dunes. It stretched for miles. We also took a football to play around with, so it was a most enjoyable day. So much so, in fact, that we went on a number of future occasions to the very same spot.

During the last stage of the route to Sidi Faroush we travelled for a number of kilometres through delightful wooded country not unlike the New Forest. There was a picnic area halfway along this drive called Robinson's Cafe with tables set out under the trees and on the wide grass verge. There were also swings and seesaws for young children. We formed a habit of making a halt there on the outward trip, picking up lemonade and anything else we fancied and then called again, to drop off the empties on the return journey.

About 20 April we heard that most of the Regiment were to have seven days' leave at a Rest Camp somewhere on the coast. Names were taken of those wishing to go, so all our party except Charlie did so and I persuaded Alex to put in for it too. Quite a number of the 'boys', mostly tank crew, had spent an Easter leave up at the winter resort of Chrea so they were among those to remain in Camp.

It transpired about this time that our SQMS's dog, named Judy, gave birth to puppies. 'Buck' Jones, our Squadron Sergeant Major, claimed one of these puppies. His chosen one was a pretty little thing with black spots on a white body so, of course, Spot was its name – and it proved to be a big spot of bother too! Before long it was discovered that Spot had rabies and so it had to be shot.

Now the fun started! It appeared on orders that anyone who had been licked, bitten, or otherwise engaged in action with the dog known as Spot was to report sick at once. What a golden opportunity for scroungers! Yes, I expect some had fancied a licking. All these people totalling about 16, including the Sergeant Major, the QM plus his staff and my pal Alex, had to attend a clinic in Algiers one morning a fortnight for 14 injections.

Leg pulling a-plenty followed. For instance, when a sufferer approached a non-sufferer a sound of barking was heard, followed by a request to see the injection spots. Another time, those sufferers who were billeted in the wine factory barracks returned from Algiers to find large meat bones suspended on strings over their beds. The cookhouse was suspected of supplying the bones but, as they announced with very straight faces, "There are no bones in bully beef". Anyway, the sufferers had some compensation in being excused duties. The injections, however, prevented them from going to the Rest Camp with us on 24 April and so I was disappointed not to have Alex's company.

The Rest Camp was at Sarouf, about 20 kilometres east of Algiers. It was a very big established Camp spread along the shore or low cliffs with mostly row after row of patrol tents, each row having a name board such as 'The Strand' and so on. The tents were also in blocks with each block having the name of an English city. We soon discovered this Camp was run and organised by an Army Chaplain and at our welcome meeting he proved a very cheerful Parson indeed.

Our party took over one of the tents in Cardiff block. We had quite a restful time of it. I was mainly in the company of Jock and 'Nix' for bathing and in and around the many canteens. A fleet of vehicles was running to and from Algiers like a bus service but Jock, 'Nix' and I only went in one afternoon for a few hours.

On 29 April a C Squadron lorry turned up at the Rest Camp soon after breakfast time. This came to 'round up' the football team because that afternoon was to be the semi-final of the Divisional Knockout. The date had been brought forward by one week and C Squadron had won their way into this semi-final. I had not played in the last four matches but because of the uncertainty of rounding everyone up I was asked to go along.

The lorry left the Camp packed with players and also those who had decided to come along to watch. We travelled the 20 odd kilometres back to St Marguerite where we all had lunch. The game was on our pitch and we just managed a 1-0 win. Alex watched the game and from him I learnt that he and others of the rabies party were departing for the Rest Camp at 16:00 hours. I made a quick change and just made that lorry with Alex, back to Sarouf. The remainder of the team and others from the Rest Camp did not travel back until after dinner. So it transpired that Alex and I did have a couple of days together after all.

As the month of May came in, so we went into our KD uniforms. We also recommenced taking the anti-malaria tablets and were issued with mosquito nets.

CHAPTER SIXTEEN

GOODBYE TO NORTH AFRICA
May 1944

These first two weeks of May were very busy ones because it became known that a move was imminent and a move by sea at that. Again, rumours of a return to England spread rapidly and were not dampened when tanks and vehicles left for the docks at Algiers. Our vehicle was fully loaded when Jack drove it off to the docks. A large scale of men to vehicles was required for the purpose of guarding at the docks and also on the transport ships. The rest of the Regiment left St Marguerite in possession of standard Army kit on 13 May and travelled by troop carriers to a Transit Camp near Blida.

Blida lay nestled at the foot of the Atlas Mountains at a point directly below the village of Chrea, the winter resort of the well-to-do French people of Algeria. The Transit Camp was about one and a half kilometres out of town on the main west road. Here large patrol tents were set out in rows and blocks. Each block seemed to have a Regiment of our Brigade. Our party had our own tent so we were comfortable despite the space taken up by our kit bags, valises, haversacks and so forth. Sanitary and washing arrangements were good and there was a huge hut that served as the canteen.

We were told to have an easy time during the few days

we were there; however, these few days turned out to be ten. Towards the end we found ourselves kept occupied during the mornings with lectures. A Staff Officer who was an authority on oil and petrol gave one lecture I well recall. We learnt from him the full story of these vital war items and how they were transported in many ways to the war fronts. Another morning we were called on Parade and loaded into trucks to run into Blida where we were quickly marched into a cinema and shown the film 'Tunisian Victory', followed by a couple of Donald Duck cartoons.

During the ten days we were allowed to go into the town between the hours of 12:00 and 20:00 so Alex and I went on several afternoons, going to a club for tea and cake and walking around the town or into the park. One day we partook of a haircut each and on another went in for a hot bath.

At the Transit Camp, speculation was rife as to our destination and some felt very strongly that we should be going home for a time in any case. Our Fitter Sergeant, 'Blondy' Osborne, had always said with a grin and shrug of the shoulders, "Oh, we'll be home in '47", but at this time he became most confident of us going home before his own deadline.

Out of the 'Flying Fitters' and our party, Bud, Frank and 'Nix' had gone with the tanks and vehicles and would travel onwards to our next destination with them. 24 May was our movement day and 10:30 hours saw us all lined up in Squadrons ready to march the two kilometres to Blida railway station. Our kit bags and bedrolls had earlier that day been loaded into lorries and were being taken direct to the dockside. We, however, had to undertake the march carrying packs, haversacks, gas kit and personal arms, in fact, full Marching Order. Of all the glorious sunny days we had spent in Africa it happened, this particular morning, to rain. The rain simply teemed down as we marched at ease towards Blida. We all wore our gas capes over both our kit and ourselves and I guess we looked a lot like washed-out, hump-backed vagabonds.

The railway stations in North Africa were for the most part nothing but a plot of land where the miles of single track divided into two. Blida, however, boasted a couple of short platforms at each track and one of these had a covering. Two of our Squadrons managed to manoeuvre into a place under this roof but C Squadron, bringing up the rear, was left to dance to the raindrops at the High Street level-crossing gates. After a while the rain eased and then stopped altogether. We soon unloaded our burdens and found we had kept surprisingly dry, except for the backs of our shirts that were damp with perspiration.

Our special train was eventually marshalled into position at the platform after much whistle blowing, shunting and opening and shutting of crossing gates. One might have expected this train to be like those all-corridor express trains of Blighty, but no. Picture a train of box trucks, or goods trucks, each one bearing the notice "Eight Horses or 40 Men" and being drawn by a couple of huge American locomotives. Fortunately we were not bundled in quite as badly as 40 to a truck so, in the one in which I found myself, there were only 25 of us. Everybody seemed excited, almost like a Sunday school outing, as the train started away.

Later we settled down to eat our haversack rations for lunch and then exercised our voices in songs old and new. We cheered as our train rattled through Boufarik across the familiar level crossing and it was not long before we were approaching the outskirts of Algiers. As the train steamed slowly along the waterfront at Algiers we were all eyes for the ships. There were three big ones docked at the quayside and several others out in the harbour.

Another hour and our kit bags and bedrolls had been sorted out and we were seated on these while waiting to board the ship. A cigarette issue of 50 per man was handed round and it was then that we learnt, unofficially, that we were bound for Italy. We were hurried up the gangplank and through the iron doors at the ship's side, along narrow corridors and up the main stairway, to our home on No. 2 deck for a few days.

We got settled in and soon had a hot meal, with tea, and fruit salad for afters. It seemed that we were on the main deck of the ship, since a short corridor and a lounge took us to the open deck near the bow and here the remainder of that day was whiled away. A party of Ship's Stewards and Ship's Cooks had a large crowd of spectators to watch them playing Deck Quoits.

Our ship was one of the peacetime Union Castle line, the 17,000-ton 'Durban Castle'. It had one very large squat funnel. Some part of that first evening on board was spent watching the hustle aboard the other two large ships. These were the 'Winchester Castle' and a French liner called 'Isle de France'. Presently, the 'Isle de France' was tugged out into the bay and in its place steamed a pure white hospital ship named 'Somersetshire'. On our ship loudspeakers were installed so all the while we were able to listen to music or news. The loudspeakers were also used to give ship's orders and to give warning to take cover or go to the lifebelt stations. These practise orders were carried out each day. The ship also carried a few anti-aircraft guns and a barrage balloon rode the sky above its stern.

We awoke the next day, 25 May, to find that we were under-way but the African coast remained in sight. The other two ships mentioned previously were also in the small convoy, as also were a few cargo vessels. Two Destroyers sailed protectively out in the open sea. This day was spent between the open main deck, one or other of the lounges, or the canteen. Also time was passed looking at the well-stocked windows in the row of shops on the main deck. She was indeed a lovely ship. All the woodwork was of polished oak and the canteens and lounges had oak panelling with basket chairs and settees. The toilets too were superb having one wall completely mirrored.

All that day we kept in sight of the coast and on the morning of 26 May sighted Bizerte. For most of the day, Alex and I were on the top deck changing our spot many times in order to keep in the shade, for the sun boiled down and the Mediterranean Sea was like a blue pond. Our ship had a steady, sleepy roll, otherwise we would not have known she was moving. Indeed we had to think of movement to even notice the roll. Towards dusk we seemed to be leaving the coast and so Africa disappeared from sight and it was noticed that our ship began to pick up speed.

Quite early on the morning of 27 May we sighted land

to our east and one of the ship's crew told us it was Sicily. We only passed the western tip of this island and it looked just a line of rugged cliffs.

Soon now we entered the Bay of Naples, passing very close to some smaller islands on which we could plainly see many villas dotted amongst the wooded slopes and along the coastline of little beaches. At the same time Mount Vesuvius came into view. Objects on the land each side became more and more clear the nearer we got into port. Italians in rowing boats were out in the Bay by the dozen. They came to meet the ships and beg from the passengers anything they might throw. The sea was very calm, otherwise these boats would not have dared to come within shouting distance of the big ships, although we had slowed speed and were just crawling into the port of Naples.

We sailed into the harbour all in line ahead and by now could see the much bombed-out docks and buildings. In the water many ships lay wrecked. In front of us the 'Isle de France' docked alongside a battered hospital ship.

Any Question relating to your pay or any other matter must be addressed to the Officer Commanding.........................

Army Form B 295A
(Lifts of 50)

at*...................
* To be filled in by the Officer granting the furlough.

No. 40

N.B.—This furlough, if found, should be handed to the Police.

Corps. 10th Royal Hussars

Company, Battery, etc. "C"

FURLOUGH

STAMP OF ISSUING OFFICE

No. 7919770. Rank. Tpr. Name. Crocker, V.

has permission to be absent from his quarters, from 16/8/42

to 22/8/42 and leave to proceed to Cairo

No advance is to be made to him on any account without previous reference to the Captain of his Company, etc.

Station. Field

Date. 16/8/42

Major

Lieut.-Col. Commanding.

1. Furlough signed by Major Errington, C.O. of Squadron in August 1942, who was wounded at Alamein and did not rejoin the Regiment.

2. Author's close pal, Alex Watts, Christmas Day 1943.

3. Army pal, Len Goring, in North Africa December 1943.

131

4. The author outside the shanty at St Marguerite, North Africa, March 1944.

5. Jack Usher, the party joker, and Jock Spiers in front of the technical stores lorry, St Marguerite, North Africa.

6. A tank and crew wait at the railhead near Caserta. Author, 2nd left, had been ordered to travel with the tanks.

7. Spring of 1944 – a day on the beach at Sidi Faroush, North Africa. Back row from the left, Frank Heath, Harry Ainsworth and Charlie Slark. Front, Jock Spiers and author.

8. Studio photo of author taken in Rome, 4th April 1945 on his son Colin's 6th birthday.

FRIDAY AUGST 31

Dearest love,

Arrived by air this evening, landing in Cornwall. Am travelling all night to a DEPT. in Yorkshire, via London, + hope to be home in a day or so.

This is being written at Newquay + I expect to post it en-route. Everything O-K + hope same with you.

Nice English drizzle Rain to greet us.

love Jim

X X

9. Postcard home, written at Newquay on landing back in England in 1945.

10. Author's pal, Alex Watts on his Wedding Day, 15th September 1945.

TENTH ROYAL HUSSARS ASSOCIATION.

FORM OF REGISTRATION.

1. Number *7919770* Rank *L/Cpl.* Name (in full) *Vincent Arthur Crocker*
2. Length of Service with the Regiment *7 years* *30·8·41* to *24·8·45*
3. Date of Enlistment *3·10·40.* Date of Transfer to Reserve *Python*
4. Date of Discharge *Aug 45.* Reason for Discharge *Python*
5. Character on leaving Regiment *Exemplary.*
6. Place of Birth *Bristol, England.* Date of Birth *17·6·1908.* Age *37*
7. Present Height *5'7"* Present Weight *138 lbs.*
8. Medals (if any) Wounds (if any)
9. Pension (if any)
10. Married or Single *Married.*
11. Present Age of Wife *36.* Wife's employment before Marriage *School Teacher.*
    How many Children *one.* State Ages *6.*
12. Would you accept a situation for man and wife
13. Were you an Officer's Servant. If so, how long?
14. Were you a Mess Waiter. If so, how long?
15. Can you Drive a Single or Pair?
16. Can you Drive a Motor? *Yes.*
17. Do you understand Gardening and Country Work in General?
18. Trade before Enlistment *Storekeeper.*
19. Employment now required (a choice of three should be given) :— *Ok for employment.*
20. Town, Country, or District preferred
21. Address *20 Oberon Ave. Whitehall, Bristol 5.*
22. Certificate of Education
23. Religion *Cong.*
24. Address of last Employer *J. S. Fry & Sons, Ltd. Chocolate & Cocoa Man. SOMERDALE NR. BRISTOL*

C.O.'s Remarks :— *exemplary. Has done the job of Squadron technical storeman in a reliable and efficient manner for several years. A good cricketer.* *W. Kaye.* LIEUT.-COLONEL. COMMANDING 10th ROYAL HUSSARS

Italy 24 Aug 45 TO BE RETAINED.

Notice must be given to the Secretary of result of any offer of employment whether refused or accepted, otherwise nothing further can be offered.

The Secretary should be notified of any change of address.

Association Address :—
322, SCOTT ELLIS GARDENS,
ST. JOHN'S WOOD, N.W.8.

11. Form of Registration. The CO's remarks read – "Has done the job of Squadron Technical Storeman in a reliable and efficient manner for several years. A good cricketer."

PART III

ITALY

CHAPTER SEVENTEEN

ARRIVAL IN NAPLES

May 1944

There was an Italian cruiser lying on her side in the docks and it was against her that our ship came to a mooring on this late morning of 27 May. We all reached the quay down a gangway that had been erected along the length of the cruiser's side. Eventually our kit bags and bedrolls were dumped into heaps and a small party was detailed to stay with these until transport arrived. The rest of us were paraded and told we would have to march six kilometres owing to lack of transport. It was a boiling hot day too.

We started off marching in good order through some of Naples' main streets where the local population stood to watch us pass. We were allowed to whistle, and so marched to "Pack up your troubles" and other similar

139

Army favourites. Maybe the most popular marching tune, which we sang as well as whistled was "Roll me over in the clover".

Naples had some very fine buildings and the main roads were wide and good but the dockside impression of it being an unkempt and uncared for city remained. Maybe the bombed and damaged buildings helped to create that impression but also the majority of the homes and people seemed of a poor class. The Italian people are by nature dark and this may have given a false impression of dirtiness. There was nothing in the town to compete with the beauty of the bay.

During our march we passed dozens of open stalls on the streets selling and displaying many fruits including oranges and lemons but our mouths just had to water, for we marched on. Presently, like the Duke of York, we marched up a very steep hill and from the top had a grand view of the bay and coastline around to Vesuvius. Here the order was given to "Fall Out" for a 20-minute break. My first need was met by drinking my bottle dry, then I joined the rest seated on the rough grass verge of the roadside and enjoyed a 'fag'. Alex was not on this march, he being lucky enough to be detailed with the kit bag party.

Soon after our rest open country was reached and at last we came to the Transit Camp. There was no provision made for our arrival for we found a bare field devoid of nearly all grass but containing some trees from which there were wires suspended bearing grape vines. We sat in disorderly fashion in the shade of the trees around this field for a long time before a couple of heavy lorries arrived with tentage. Tents were allocated out and we had to set about erecting them. There was some grumbling about having to do this following the rather long march but it was pointed out that this Camp should have been made ready to receive us, so there must have been a slip-up somewhere. We heard later, true or not, that we should have sailed to Taranto and that was why nothing was prepared for us here. What we did know to be a fact was that all our own transport, tanks included, was waiting to be collected at Taranto docks.

Our party managed to arrange to have a tent to ourselves and soon a lorry arrived loaded with rations. In no time at all a stack of bread was piled up on the ground so our hungry appetites were quickly appeased. This spot was near a little township called Afrikola.

Next morning a number of our echelon drivers left by road for Taranto, this being 28 May. Leave was granted for anyone to go into Naples but those who went would have to make their own way there and back. Alex and I decided to go after lunch and we found it easy to pick up a lift on the main highway running past the Camp.

A further letter from an old friend, Norman Anderson, had informed me that he was now in the Naples area, so Alex and I kept our eyes open for No. 104 Hospital. Norman's brother and sister had married my wife's sister and brother, so there would be much family news to share if we could meet. There were a number of services hospitals in Naples but we did not see a sign for No. 104.

We had a pleasant few hours roaming around the town

and also had refreshments at a large NAAFI, one of the best of its kind that I had seen. On the second floor was a relaxing lounge with armchairs and settees that one could sink right into, whilst in a corner a trio played enchanting music.

Alex and I were seated at a table about to enjoy our second ice cream, when an unknown British Tommy came up and said, "See from your cap badge you are 10th Royal Hussars". We said, "Yes, that's right". He went on to say, "Do you happen to know a Lance Corporal Graham who is in C Squadron?" We, of course, both cried, "Yes" and added, "He is a Driver Mechanic and we know him very well indeed". He then disclosed he was 'Nix' Graham's younger brother and they had not seen one another for four years. His Regiment had recently been withdrawn from the line and he was in Naples for a short period of leave. Unfortunately, we had to tell him that 'Nix' was with the Regiment's transport over at Taranto and so he would be unable to meet him. We talked together for a good half hour and came away with a message for 'Nix'. It is sad to relate that they didn't meet up and less than three months after this 'Nix' had a letter from home telling him that this brother had been killed in action in Italy.

During the evening after our return from Naples, we were talking in the tent and Bill Howe (of 'Flying Fitters') asked if I had found out where the hospital was. I told him we had been unable to discover its whereabouts. Bill then said, "There's a hospital up here, just over the other side of Afrikola. What number did you say it was?" I said, "104". Bill said, "That's it, that's it, it's the one in Afrikola. Follow this track through some vines until you strike another road, turn left and then take the first on the right – only 10 minutes' walk". Apparently Bill, Charlie and the others had walked over to a canteen in Afrikola in the afternoon and Bill had then noticed the 104 Hospital sign on the corner of the right-hand turn.

The next day, 29 May, as soon as lunch was over Alex and I took the track that led to the little town and soon came upon the hospital turning. There was a large white modern building standing in its own grounds bearing the Red Cross sign. In the grounds stood a large number of tents in neat rows (we learnt later it was one of Italy's modern schools and playing fields). There was a five-bar gate, also in white, at the entrance and a Military Policeman stood guarding it. It was this MP who directed us to Norman Anderson's tent, which happened to be one of the first along the track.

Thus for the first time I knew the thrill of meeting a civvy street friend whilst abroad. I introduced Alex as a pal of mine and we talked unceasingly for an hour then took a walk to the canteen in the town. Alex and I went back to Camp for dinner and, as Alex was down for guard duty that night, I went alone to see Norman in the evening. We chatted for several hours over a mug of tea and a couple of cakes in a corner of the canteen. We made arrangements to meet the following afternoon and to stay for dinner at the hospital. This we did and afterwards joined with the hospital soccer team that was conveyed to a nearby town for a match. Norman played a good game, at least as far as we could see through the dust storm caused as players ran about or kicked the ball. This was still in May mark

143

you! Norman, with two of his friends and I, walked back to Afrikola where we had a last little chat and then a farewell handshake. It was already known that we were to move on the next day but we promised to try to meet up again if our paths crossed.

CHAPTER EIGHTEEN

MATERA & GRAVINA
May to June 1944

On 31 May at 10:00 hours we paraded in Marching Order and started off for the little railway station at Afrikola which was only a short march away. Our train was of exactly the same type as the one we travelled in from Blida to Algiers. In our truck we had 20 men, a little fewer this time because it would be necessary for each of us to have a sleeping space. Before our journey commenced rations for two days were issued to each truck party.

When the train was on the move it kept up a fair speed but at the many junction stations it seemed usual to have a stop for an hour or so. This may have been partly due to the fact that there was only a single line working and a changeover in places from steam engines to electric. The electric trains ran off overhead wires carried by elaborate steel poles and arms at about every 30 yards. Priority was probably being given to goods, or gun and tank carrying trains. No trains conveying civilians were running at this time and the few who obtained special permits had to find room on Army trains.

In one way the long halts were a blessing since it gave time for meals and brew-ups and for having a wash at a station pump or wayside water pump. Our box truck was near the engine and so a few times we snatched a 'Jitty' (quick) brew-up obtaining near boiling water from our American engine driver.

Of the towns we passed, I remember only Benevento. Soon after that a number of us played Rummy for a long spell. It was another game altogether trying to get sorted out for sleeping but in the end I think most slept for at least a few hours.

At about 14:00 on 1 June we ran into a small town called Altamura and it was here that we de-trained. There were a number of our Regiment's lorries lined up outside the station and in C Squadron line we found Frank, 'Bud' and 'Nix' each ready to drive a lorry. We were all conveyed the 20 odd kilometres to Matera, a town that lay inland about 45 kilometres from Taranto in the heel of Italy.

We pulled up at a small square which appeared to be in the oldest part of the town and were very soon bustled into a very ancient looking building. This place turned out to be a rambling old monastery school, as we discovered whilst having to carry all our kit through the long flag-stoned corridors and up flights of stone stairways.

The entrance to the place looked quite imposing with its tower and wide stone steps leading to a well designed double doorway. At the side of the building, on entrance door level, ran a veranda that overlooked a deep gorge. We came to know this by its proper name, 'The Grotto'. Inside we found the rooms very large and able to accommodate a troop (about 15 men) comfortably. Each room had a long wide table and an ante-room of washbasins and toilets.

It transpired that our party and the 'Flying Fitters' only spent one night in this building, for next morning we had to move to where a vehicle park was going to be set up. This was in a big field just outside of Matera and about two kilometres from the monastery school where most of the Regiment remained billeted.

Our party and the 'Flying Fitters' each had our large patrol tents. The other Squadrons' trade personnel went to this field, as did the LAD. The B Squadron mobile cooks' lorry also went there to provide meals for this group. We considered ourselves lucky to be away from the Regiment in this way for it enabled us to escape both parades and early morning reveilles.

By the morning of 3 June we had really become settled in an out-of-the-way corner of this field and as only part of the wheeled vehicles had so far arrived there was not much to do. About mid-day Alex came down for the 15 cwt Bedford truck used mostly as a runabout vehicle, for which he seemed to have become the established driver. Captain Lloyd of our Squadron was returning to England on a staff job and so Alex was to take him and his kit to Naples.

The field in which we were camped was adjoining the main road to Taranto and it sloped slightly away to a corner. We were in this far corner almost against a low stone wall, beyond which was a large field of corn. From the tent we could see a view of rolling hills, some covered in waving corn, interspersed with groves of cherry trees. In the early mornings with the sun shining from a cloudless blue sky I would wash and shave wearing only shorts and plimsolls. The air was very still and I used to pause to listen to the songs of the farm workers in the nearby fields.

During the evening of 4 June, George and I had a ramble around the countryside. The roads and lanes were thick with dust so we kept to the fields as much as possible. We came across a quarry and saw men cutting out large blocks of stone with only a saw. The stone must have been quite soft and was golden-coloured like Bath stone. About four kilometres from our Camp we bumped into a couple of C Squadron officers. They were out rambling too and carried their tunics over their arms and had shirt sleeves well rolled up. We stayed awhile chatting and they explained that they were looking for a stream in which to fish. George and I continued on our circular route and next came to a farm where a man and boy were busy in the garden. We offered greetings "Buongiorno" but could not understand what the 'old boy' went on to say. However, a few cigarettes seemed to please him no end. We arrived back at the tent as darkness was falling, each with our cap full of cherries.

5 June was much about the same sort of day, with George and I going on another evening ramble but in a different direction.

About mid-morning on 6 June a rumbling noise which grew louder and louder told us of the arrival of the Regiment's tanks from Taranto. Soon after they had all pulled in and we had chatted to one and another of the drivers (they were not fully crewed) about Taranto and the trip up, we all heard a big slice of news. Someone came down from the Regiment's billets at Matera and told us that a news cable from HQ was pinned up on the notice board simply stating that the Second Front had commenced and that the allies had invaded France in the early hours that day.

There was, of course, a gathering of the gang; we talked much over this great news, speculated as to which part of the coast had been invaded and wondered how things were going. News over the air was very difficult to get during daytime in Matera but though Charlie could not get the 13:00 news on his little set, the 'Flying Fitters' did on theirs and we all heard this with much eagerness and excitement. There was no rambling that evening, all being too keen to hear the various news bulletins. The 20:45 European news was the last we heard that night. 7 June was another day of invasion talk and we again listened-in to all the news up until 20:45, glad that things seemed to be going well.

This period of time was uplifting to everyone since not only had the Second Front started but here in Italy good progress was being made too. The mountains around Cassino held by the enemy had been a stumbling block for some months but, in May, Cassino had at last been taken and on 4 June Rome had also fallen into our hands. So Matera was becoming a place for hearing some wonderful news and we were the happier because of it.

The weather was still grand when 8 June dawned and this day, being a day off, quite a large number of the Regiment went in lorries to Bari for a swim. None of our party went, however, as there were some modifications to be done on the tanks though personally I had a lazy day at home!

In the evening after dinner George, Jock, 'Nix' and I decided on a walk up into town. The two kilometres up to Matera was a steady climb all the way. The only things of note on the way were a convent school on the right hand side standing in its own grounds and on the left a row of poor-looking houses. Then as we approached the town we noticed a long white concrete wall, in the centre of which were large iron gates that were wide open. We took a peep in and found ourselves looking down from the flat roof of a grandstand on to a dry and dusty football pitch. There was some concrete terracing along the sides and up at the far end. A day later we saw part of a game between Matera and Altamura which was evidently a local derby judging by the high-spirited mixed crowd and the scraps on the field. For the first time I saw a player come off and another fresh chap go on in his place. Substitutes were allowed over there!

Having had our peep we then strolled over the railway level crossing (only a light railway) and entered the town. We at once noticed that there was something out of the ordinary taking place. Most of the houses had colourful banners hanging from the upstairs windows. On reaching the square in the middle of the High Street we were held up by crowds of people lining each side of the square and a couple of the streets leading off. We enquired of several troops, "What's on?" and eventually learnt that it was the celebration of Corpus Christi and that a procession of the RC Church was somewhere about. Jock and 'Nix' said, "Trust us to bump into something like this" and were not a bit keen to wait for the procession as George and I were.

To us it appeared a very strange do. First came a number of Italian Police wearing their dark green uniforms and large cocked hats, followed by children from tiny tots to older girls and boys with everyone dressed in white. Then, in the following order, came the widows dressed in black complete with veils; monks; nuns and priests. There were a number of banners and gilded crosses held aloft. The senior priest walked very slowly (for he was a very old man) under a four-posted canopy, which was elaborately golden gilded with lighted candles set in numerous places. All these people were muttering scripture or prayers. As the senior priest passed along every Italian local knelt on the pathway and crossed their breast. At our viewpoint there was a group of young children watching and they did not kneel as the senior priest approached. One of the lesser-lights of priesthood broke from the procession and, coming up to the youngsters, bade them to kneel and cross their breasts. It was clear to us that the RC Church was very powerful here in Italy.

After viewing the procession we turned into a cafe and enjoyed ices before calling at the Regiment's billets for any mail and to talk with some of the 'boys'. We later enjoyed the steady walk down the hill to our Camp.

9 and 10 June were far busier days so we stayed in Camp and satisfied ourselves with listening-in to all the evening news. Next day 11 June saw the start of the big scheme which involved the tanks and A Echelon. These vehicles, fully crewed, pulled out of the field around mid-morning. Our party being part of B Echelon remained where we were for the time being. Thus we were left in the corner of the field with only our store lorry and a few others to look after. In various parts of the field the three other Squadrons' store lorries and those forming B Echelon also remained. The 'Flying Fitters' of each Squadron had departed, as they were of course part of A Echelon.

From now on our party used our store lorry to run to and from the Matera billets for our meals but each time one of us stayed to watch the tent, etc. That person's meal was then brought back. Some of the drivers and mates of B Echelon vehicles remained at the billets, as also did the A Squadron cooks to provide our meals. The period we stayed on in this fashion was from 11 to 18 June and it was a cushy time indeed for us.

On the 13th George, 'Nix' and I planned to stay in town after the evening dinner. It was Jock's turn for tent guarding so he could not join us. We three sauntered down to the main square where we discovered the only cinema had now opened up for the troops. Nearby, too, was a NAAFI canteen established, so we blew in as we had some spare time. We had a cup of the usual NAAFI tea and were able to make one or two small purchases.

'Nix' had arranged to meet an Italian student with whom he had become acquainted so, when it neared the time, we ceased talking at our NAAFI table and went to a road junction where, between the fork-roads, there was a small green park. Here 'Nix' spotted his student pal seated on one of the benches and George and I were soon introduced. The student could speak English fairly well and he introduced himself as 'Tony', short for Antonio. Tony conducted us around the grotto part of the old town and also into the Cathedral. Later on he took us to his home where we were able to meet his parents and it was midnight when we got back to our tent.

On the evening of the 15th I was at the tent alone, the others having decided to go to the pictures in Matera. My hope was to catch up on some letter writing but two young boys put in an appearance and we started talking or, rather, trying to. I invited the boys into the tent and soon discovered their names and something about them. This was not because I could understand their tongue but rather that they could speak a few phrases of English. One said his name was Domenica and went on, "Italian – Domenica, English – Sunday". The other said, "Italian – Michel, English – Michael". They asked my name, I said "Vincent". "Ah!" said Domenica, "English – Vincent, Italian – Vincenzo". I recited the English alphabet, "A, B, C", etc and they tried to repeat it. Eventually they managed it save for one or two letters they found difficult to say. They then recited the Italian alphabet which I tried to learn but I was not very good. I did manage, however, to count from 1 to 20 in Italian. We chatted away the whole evening and I discovered they were both 14 years old and attended school superior (secondary school). I found they simply could not say the 'th' sound as in 'mother' but their favourite phrase in English was, "Just a little bit".

These boys turned up again on the next two evenings but on the 17th (my birthday) I had been very bilious all day and so was in bed when they came.

Gravina

On the afternoon of 18 June we moved ten kilometres along with the rest of B Echelon to a spot near a place called Gravina. Here all the B Echelons of the Brigade parked up in a cornfield and there was little work to be done since most wheeled vehicles were new at St Marguerite and mileages had been kept low. It was interesting to watch the binding machine at work on the corn. This was guided by a man leading a couple of horses. The machine cut the corn and at frequent intervals threw out a bound bundle.

Our tanks, all this while, had been on the special scheme which involved working with Infantry on close country work. The word 'close' related to areas where woods, hills, trees, farms and outbuildings afforded plenty of cover, such as abounds in Italy.

On 21 June, three days after our move, an urgent call came for every 3-ton lorry in the Brigade to be made available. This meant petrol, ammunition, stores and everything being off-loaded and dumps made in the field. Our lorry came under this order so, having our patrol tent erected, we stripped the lorry which was a good morning's work and placed the metal bins and stores in the tent. Our beds had to squeezed up together but we managed.

At 16:00 a long convoy of lorries, with 1st and 2nd drivers, were ready for the special ferrying of petrol from Taranto to Rome and the forward area. When it came to it, the convoy remained static until next morning the 22nd and moved off eventually with the exception of the lorries of the 10th Royal Hussars. We wondered why as we worked away fitting-out our lorry again, with the others of the 10th doing the same. This was cleared up for us when on the 23 June we moved up together as a Regiment to the spot where the tanks were leaguered.

Lieutenant Colonel Kaye lost no time in giving us the 'griff' and this was to the effect that our Regiment had been selected to link up with the 1st British Infantry

Division, since that Division had done no training in the new technique of working with armoured support. Squadrons of the Regiment would be allotted to various Brigades and we would gain benefit from the training together. We would be attached to them for one month and it would be a month of hard training. However, we would not mind this training as we would be stationed within a few miles of Rome and he promised everyone would have the chance of a day or two's leave in the city.

Next morning 24 June our tanks and crews departed on transporters for Bari where they were to join a train to be transported up to the Rome area. For some reason Charlie, 'Nix' and George departed with the tanks, as also did the 'Flying Fitters' with their armoured car. The echelon of lorries forming the Regimental convoy stayed static until dusk on the 27th when they formed up in close leaguer along a lane ready for an early move.

CHAPTER NINETEEN

GRAVINA TO ROME

June to July 1944

Reveille was at 04:00 hours on the 28 June and the convoy moved away promptly at 05:00 in the order HQ, A, B, C Squadrons. Order for the move was 'best possible speed, no overtaking' and each driver was given a route card for the day's trip. This was what our route card stated – 'Route 96 to Gravina, Irsina, Tolve. Route 7 to Potenza, Victri, Auletta. Route 19 to Eboli, Battipaglia. Route 18 to Mercatello, Salerno'. It was a wonderful scenic trip amid the mountains nearly all the way. Tolve, in particular, was a town right on a mountain top, to which we travelled up and up, the road twisting and turning like some huge snake. Most of the roads on this journey were minor cross-country ones, not very straight, not very wide and rough with very dusty surfaces.

It was close to 19:00 hours when the convoy concluded the day's run of 150 kilometres by leaguering for the night right on the beach at Salerno. It provided the chance for most of the troops to have a dip in the briny during the hour or so before sunset and it was the best way of washing off the grime and dust of the road.

Next day, 29 June, reveille was at 05:30 hours with each Squadron moving off at half-hour intervals from 06:00 hours. This was to minimise congestion travelling through the Naples area. The route card read 'Route 18 to Pompei, Naples. Route 87 to Caserta. Then Highway 6 – Capua, Vairano (lunch stop). Continue Highway 6 – Cassino, Arce, Ceprano, Frosinone, Ferentino.' This was another highly interesting day's travel. Pompeii at the foot of Vesuvius, Naples where our party managed a little halt to buy oranges and plums, and passing the very field at Afrikola where we had camped on arrival in Italy.

Passing through Naples the convoy, despite leaving at intervals, became very mixed up. We in our vehicle, for instance, must have taken a shorter route at some point because we arrived at the big road junction at Caserta before any other of the Regiment's lorries. Something new to the Regiment since landing in Italy were two motorcycle Military Police to guide and patrol convoys. One of our MPs, Corporal Eric Wyles, was on duty at this point and he flagged us down and told us to pull in and wait. It was some 15 or 20 minutes before the convoy started coming through but eventually we took up our rightful place.

After the lunch break at Vairano we were all eyes for Cassino and the Monastery Hill where there had been much fierce fighting over several months before the allied break-through. The place was in an awful pickle, just mounds of stone and rubble and yards and yards of white tape marking a rough track through, with signs of mines, mines, mines everywhere. It was a touch of very cold humour to read a large sign on one big heap of rubble. It stated, "Continental Hotel – Under New Management". Having driven about another 150 kilometres we spent the night near Ferentino, leaguering on a wide strip of common land adjoining the highway.

On the 30 June reveille was at 06:00 hours and we had an early start, continuing on Route 6 passing Valmontone. Soon after this we left Route 6 and cut across country to the southwest on a minor road and, after some distance, climbed a steep hill. Eventually from this higher level two spectacular sights became visible. One was the distant city of Rome with its buildings showing up sparkling white in the blazing sunshine. The other sight was to the left where, lying deep under the hillside and surrounded by wooded slopes, was the bluest stretch of water I think I had ever seen. Set as it was, surrounded by wooded slopes. It looked a dream.

The road gradually dipped down and down until we came to the water's edge and then ran along its bank for about one kilometre. There was a narrow stretch of black sandy beach all around this part of the lake and there were many troops enjoying the bathing. This was Lake Albano and soon we came to the much-damaged little town of Albano. Very shortly this minor road joined up to Highway 7.

Highway 7 was the coast road running between Rome and Naples known as the Appian Way. It was constructed by the early Romans and had been in existence for centuries. It joined Highway 6 at the big road junction at Caserta near Naples where we had to stop and await the convoy. From the heights above Albano we had seen Highway 7 sloping away as straight as a die for the 20 kilometres into Rome.

We travelled to within six kilometres of the city and then cut across country again until reaching the Rome-Anzio road, where we leaguered up.

During this trip up from Naples it was noticed that Highway 6 was choc-a-bloc with supply convoys, tanks, transporters, guns and all sorts, with everything going the one way – north. I believe Highway 7, at least in part, must have been the route south to Naples. We crossed the main railway line at several points near Rome and noticed that the retreating 'Jerry' had left it in a right pickle. It was electrified but overhead wires were dangling, carrying-posts and arms were down or bent out of shape and the lines were torn up for yards at a stretch. The banking was blown away in places and most bridges were beyond use.

Having reached our new area in early afternoon we found the countryside to be rather undulating. From the higher points, the glistening white buildings of Rome could always be sighted and turning slowly – right about turn as the soldier does – we could see the skyline of the Apennine mountains, then the heights of Albano and lastly the reflecting dazzle of the brilliant sun on the Mediterranean.

Each Squadron had its own area and our wheeled vehicles were in a vale between sloping hills, through which ran a small stream. A decent track led the half-mile in from the road, and the lorries were spaced out along the small hedgerow of the stream. Another Regiment had recently vacated this area and we benefited from the fact that they had neatly dammed up the stream, thus creating a small pool roughly a dozen yards in length and about five in breadth. It was deep enough at the dammed end to allow for diving.

We parked our lorry within 20 yards of the pool and erected the sham-e-ola. It was at St Marguerite in North

Africa that a number of these had been fixed on various vehicles. It consisted of a tarpaulin-like material, one side of which was made fast to the top and length of the lorry canopy. It then sloped out and down to a ridgepole carried by an upright pole at each end. End flaps were added and completed a perfect lean-to tent for four or five people. When not in use the poles were slackened from guy ropes and laid lengthways. The whole 'bag of tricks' was then rolled up to the topside of the lorry where three straps secured it. It was while our 'fitters' were fixing these up that an officer came and asked if his 'sham-e-ola' was finished. They, in surprise, said, "Sham-e-ola, what's that?" The officer said, "Oh, that lean-to tent affair". From then on the name stuck!

When we had settled down in this new spot my first job, I recall, was to wash out my travel-stained KD shirt and shorts. In the evening the pool was tried out and found to be 'just the job'.

The following day, 1 July, our tanks arrived and those of our Squadron parked in open leaguer on the hillside overlooking the little vale with the crews living in tents by the side of their tanks. The 'Flying Fitters' also arrived in the armoured car and parked up next to us. Also George, Charlie and 'Nix' rejoined us after a tiresome trip up with the tank party. During the latter part of the day, the CO passed down information to NCOs to the effect that we should be in that area for possibly five weeks and each Squadron would join up with an Infantry Regiment for a training period of two weeks.

CHAPTER TWENTY

ROME

July to August 1944

The Regiment had been able to secure suitable premises in Rome for a club. Anyone in the city on day leave (ten men from each Squadron per day would initially be allowed) could obtain a good lunch and dinner. At no other place in Rome could meals be obtained at that time. To help with expenses a charge of 80 lire (20p) would be made. Anyone meeting a friend in the city, no matter what branch of the Services, the friend would be welcome at the club. In the lounge a wine bar would be set up and opened during lunch hours and evenings. The wine bar showed such good profits that after a couple of weeks the club charge was reduced by a half!

Our Squadron was unable to join up with an Infantry Unit for a few weeks and so this period was not a busy one. True, we did a bit during the mornings but the rest of the time was spent doing our own thing. Mostly we enjoyed a dip in the pool. Our party would take the splash about mid-afternoon and perhaps stay sunbathing on the grassy bank until dinner. Dinner was, like our desert custom, still being served in the evenings around 17:30 or 18:00.

From the very start, trips commenced into Rome so George, Charlie, Jimmy and I put in for our turn on 6 July. We were up bright and early in anticipation that morning and were ready before the duty driver of the lorry. The party was away at the stated time of 08:30. The road in was a little rough and bumpy for the first few miles, it having received some attention in the advance north. However, we soon joined Highway 8 which was the main route from Rome to the city's playground on the coast, Roma Lido.

Now things began to get interesting. We first noted the tramway track running at the side of the now wide road built up several feet from road level. There were no trams running and we guessed the electric power was not yet restored. Indeed, the only traffic in Rome at this time was military except for bicycles and a type of small delivery van that appeared very popular. These were no more than three-wheeled motorbikes with a body built over and beyond the two back wheels.

Soon on the left we passed a large area covered with more recently erected sparkling white buildings and we learnt that this was to have been the scene of the Olympic Games in 1940. After this buildings appeared on each side of the road and, though there were plenty of civilians walking the pavements, there seemed to be an even greater multitude of bicycles going hither and thither.

Later we passed through a market place where there were carts by the hundred – hand carts, donkey carts, mule carts and so on, each seeming to be loaded with fruit. Then we passed under one of those large ancient archways and so into Rome's historical centre.

Soon we were in the shadow of the Colosseum and alongside the pillars of the old Roman Forum. The wide road, called Via dei Fori Imperiali, led us into a very large square called Piazza Venezia. Here was the huge Victor Emmanuel II Memorial and also the Palazzo Venezia, a rather drab-looking building for a palace, but then it was built in 1465. It was from an insignificant balcony of this palace that Mussolini, the former Duce, used to address the throng in the vast square. Now, from an imposing building across the square from Mussolini's Palace, flew the Union Jack and the Stars and Stripes. Around the smart entrance were wooden crush barriers and it was here that the Italians now gathered to watch the comings and goings of the 'big-wigs' of Allied HQ.

We travelled through the square and down another main road eventually turning in at a narrow side street. Here we alighted from the lorry for we were outside the 'Shiners' Club. We entered quite a spacious lounge and, at a desk, obtained our lunch and dinner tickets. We decided to defer a more detailed look at the club premises until returning for lunch.

Charlie and Jim made off for St Peter's Basilica but George and I thought it better to leave going over there until after lunch when we would have longer to look around. Thus, George and I sauntered off to the main road and after a little shop window gazing reached the big square through which we had recently passed. We admired for a while the huge Victor Emmanuel II Memorial, the whiteness of the stone which sparkled in the strong sunlight and the way those gilded horses and chariots right at the top showed up against the blue-ness of the sky. It did not take long for this memorial to become known by the troops as 'The Wedding Cake'.

We next wandered wonderingly among the pillars of

The Forum. One called Trojans Pillar was erected in 114AD and consisted of 34 blocks of white marble. On the top stood a bronze statue of St Peter but this had been added by one of the Popes in more recent times.

We went further on along Via dei Fori Imperiali, being interested in the stalls of the many peddlers, until we reached the amphitheatre of Imperial Rome, the wonderful ruins of the Colosseum. The building was begun in 72AD and was inaugurated by Emperor Titus in 80 AD with sports that lasted 100 days. We heard the history of the building given in typical American style by means of loudspeakers placed around the ancient arena. This is how the Yank announcer concluded his half-hour lecture, "Well boys, that's the low-down on these here ruins. I sure guess some of you feel mighty thirsty on this hot day. If you wanna drink, there's a water cart outside this office." Yes! We had a drink and a laugh too. I reckon old Titus would turn in his grave if he had known how the Yanks were expounding the history of his den.

George and I retraced our steps for lunch, purchasing en-route a good atlas from a well-stocked and high-class stationery shop. Thereafter this atlas was often studied after news bulletins. We had lunch in style at a table set for four and a trio provided some lively music throughout. Afterwards we looked around the numerous rooms and stayed a short time in one to listen to the wireless.

On coming away from the club, we somehow got into a conversation with an Italian who spoke quite good English. We soon learnt that he had spent some years in London as a waiter at a high-class hotel restaurant on Park Lane. Eventually he offered to take us to and around St Peter's. On the way we visited the Pantheon, one of the very few ancient buildings still standing in a good state of preservation. It was built by the husband of Julia, daughter of Augustus Caesar, in 27BC and was dedicated as a Temple to Mars and Venus the ancestral Gods of that family. It is the burial place of the Italian Kings and Queens and also of many artists, including Raphael. What caught my eye was the fact that it was circular like many modern halls and churches of today. The entrance doors, about 14 feet tall and 18 inches in thickness, were of solid bronze.

We walked on and came to the approaches of St Peter's, first crossing a statue-lined bridge over the Tiber. We paused to watch the many bathers who jumped or plunged in from a type of houseboat. Though it was very hot we thought we should not like to have bathed there because the Tiber was living up to its name and flowing fast.

There was so much of interest in St Peter's Basilica that to go into detail would demand almost another story. We did spend quite three hours there and went right to the top of the 493 ft dome. Everything was most awe-inspiring. Making our way back to dinner by another route we passed the Castel St Angelo and the imposing Palace of Justice.

George and I enjoyed a swell but hurried meal and this enabled us to get to an 18:00 show at a theatre taken over for the troops fairly near the club. It was a large and beautifully decorated theatre. The stalls of the ground floor were as usual but all above and around consisted of private boxes seating four people in basket-type chairs. It was our luck to be seated in one of these as the theatre was packed. The very enjoyable play was called 'Blythe Spirit' by Noel Coward and the cast included Emlyn Williams.

Our Squadron group was picked up by lorry from the club at 21:00 hours and then, with no available electricity for lighting the streets and given the fact that it was the first time in the city for all aboard, we got hopelessly lost. Eventually we found ourselves back at the club and made a fresh start which proved no more successful. In the end it was after midnight before we reached our leaguering area and those not in the cab considered this no joke, for the night air was cold for travelling in only KD slacks and shirt.

Normal days in Camp followed and I made a habit of having a before-breakfast dip in the pool. This was very pleasant too, having the pool to myself. I could only persuade George and Jock to accompany me on one occasion for they preferred lying in until breakfast was shouted up. Of course I used to have my afternoon dip too, so was taking full advantage of both pool and weather.

A nasty incident occurred soon after breakfast on 10 July. One of our tanks ran away down the hillside and crashed down a 12 foot bank into the stream. Although down-stream quite a bit, the impact of the 30-tons of steel caused vibrations which disturbed the dam of the pool so that all the water ran away. This was soon remedied but, being summertime, not much water was flowing and so the pool suffered in size.

What was far worse was the fact that the incident occurred during a wireless 'stand-to' so the wireless operator was still in the tank. Jock of our party was first on the scene because he happened to see the tank careering down the slope. It was Jock who managed to get Trooper Elliott out, and the MO and an ambulance were quickly in attendance. Jock was shocked a bit and his overalls were splattered in blood. Before dinner the news came that Elliott had died and this deflated everyone for some time. He was laid to rest in a hospital cemetery on the southern outskirts of Rome, the Regiment having laid a large wreath. He was a married man with one small daughter.

On 12 July I passed through Rome and went a little north of the city. In the truck was a tank crew, for we were going to collect a new Sherman in place of the one ditched and now unserviceable. We got fixed up after checking all that was necessary including the gun and smaller arms, serial numbers and noting the mileage done. After watching the tank depart I made for Rome and stayed a while enjoying a couple of ices before proceeding back to Camp. On the 14th of the month I made a similar trip to the same TDS (Tank Delivery Section).

The following day it became our Squadron's turn to link up with an Infantry Regiment and so we moved some six or seven miles towards Albano. Our new leaguer was amidst olive groves and here our party decided to erect the patrol tent thinking it would be cooler than the sham-e-ola and with the flysheet open it certainly was. Afternoon trips by truck to Lake Albano were allowed now and again from here and the bathing was superb, the water being so warm. It was a beautiful spot and what was unusual for us was the beach of black sand.

From this area too, another interesting day was spent in Rome, this time in the company of Alex. We visited the Sistine Chapel, world famed because of the celebrated frescoes of Michelangelo. We also went to a show in the evening.

For the first time, on one of the night exercises with the Infantry, we saw a score of searchlights used and we wondered why. It was soon discovered that their use was to create artificial moonlight and they certainly caused shadows. We thought at first it was a kind of searchlight tattoo, such as used to be held before the war at Aldershot and Tidworth. This system of lights became commonplace in future frontline areas. On 29 July at 06:00 hours we moved back to our former spot and so rejoined the remainder of the Regiment.

Next morning, 30th, there was a 'Full Parade' which was inspected by the CO. We then marched out to the Rome-Anzio road and lined up all along one side. King George VI was to pass our way and we were told 'spontaneous cheering' would break out. Well he passed by, responding to our raised caps and cheers by giving a prolonged salute. He was seated on the back hood of an open car with his feet on the seat. There were, of course, lots of other cars containing military bigwigs, press reporters and members of his entourage.

The next few days were granted as holiday and as many as wished were permitted to go into Rome either for the full day, half day or evening. Transport lorries left the Camp area at 08:30, 13:00 and 16:00 hours. On 1 August I stayed on duty alone from our party and had a really lazy day except for a little afternoon exercise in the pool.

For some time now a new vehicle had been in the charge of our party. This was a partially tracked small Carrier and each of the Squadrons had one. Charlie the electrician was in charge of this because its main purpose was carrying spare batteries and maintaining them fully charged. On 2 August all our tanks departed from the area including the 'Flying Fitters' with the armoured car and also Charlie and 'Nix' with the Carrier. As George, Jock and Jack were also instructed to travel with the tank party, this left only Frank and me with the store lorry. After the exodus of this large group Frank and I went into Rome and had a very nice time. During the evening we went to an American-run theatre and saw a play called 'The Male Animal'.

The move for the echelons came on 5 August and so we bade a fond farewell to our area and pool at 07:00 hours.

CHAPTER TWENTY-ONE

TO ORTONA

August 1944

The Route Card stated 'best possible speed via - Valmontone, Ferentino, Frosinone, Arce, Cassino, Mignano, Tavernonuvya and Alife'. The convoy travelled HQ, A, B and C Squadrons so this meant Frank and I were bringing up the rear. We had only done about 20 miles when we came upon one of our lorries in trouble. This had overheated due to a missing fan belt. After a struggle I managed to open a steel bin door in the overcrowded lorry to produce a suitable replacement. Frank soon fitted the belt but we halted a bit longer to allow the engine to cool down before moving off.

We were now an hour behind time so we tried to make this up as we travelled down Route 6 at good speed. When nearing Cassino we caught up with the Squadron but they were just moving off from a lunch stop staging point. Frank and I looked at each other and it was he who said, "We've had it" meaning of course that we would have to forgo our lunch.

Soon after the ruins of Cassino were passed we turned left off Highway 6 and our route took us along some narrow minor roads. The convoy eventually leaguered up in late afternoon having come some 100 miles southeast. Our tanks had already arrived in this area so George, Jock and Jack rejoined us.

After lunch the next day we all had to move a matter of four miles to what was considered a better spot. The tanks moved first followed by the echelons. Owing to lack of space our store lorry was not able to park in the same grove as the rest of C Echelon and so was directed to park up with the tanks. Whilst pulling into this grove we had to ride a mound of high ground on one side of a rather narrow entrance. We all bailed out except Jack who was driving and he took the mound very steadily. The lorry rocked and swayed, then over she went on to her side. She went so gently that Jack was still sitting nice and cosy in the driver's seat. We had to strip everything except store bins and then the LAD Scammel pulled her up on to her wheels again. After inspection our lorry was found to be perfectly OK and so we reloaded save for requirements for camping nearby. It was an incident that was all over in a couple of hours and we soon parked comfortably.

Next day 6 August was a busy one and I was settling down to a quiet evening when, at about 20:00, came a message for me to report at Technical Office over at nearby HQ Squadron. There I learnt of a very recent order for a move up to the east coast. The tanks would go up by rail the next evening. I was to travel with them and their crews because at the destination (Ortona) some tanks were to be handed over and would be replaced with new Sherman tanks each carrying a larger 76mm gun.

So, at 14:00 hours on the 7th, the tanks pulled out. I had my bedroll and rations with the HQ troop of C Squadron and travelled on the tank the 36 miles to Caserta rail junction. Charlie, 'Nix' and Frank were on the Carrier that was also going up by rail. One train, with B Squadron aboard, pulled out that evening. We remained at the railhead to sleep that night but next morning our tanks were loaded on to the flat trucks. The troops travelled in the normal box trucks and we made our particular one as cosy as possible and bought fruit as additional refreshment for what was likely to be a hot journey. Charlie and Co were not on this train; indeed all the Carriers were still lined up together awaiting another train.

Our train steamed out from Caserta at about 11:00 on 8 August and we reached Ortona around noon on 9 August. The last four hours of the trip afforded scenic views of coast and distant mountains as we went all along the edge of the Adriatic Sea. It did not take long to de-train at this railhead, which was almost on the beach at Ortona. This was as far north as the railway had been restored on the Adriatic side at that time. Our leaguering spot turned out to be only half a mile away on the cliff top overlooking the sea and quite near a small township through which ran the coast road.

My enquiries showed that the expected new tanks had not arrived so Alex (who had come up in the 15cwt Bedford with an officer and a small advance party) and I went down for a swim. We walked through the little town to a cliff top promenade, down a zigzag path, over a railway level crossing and so reached the beach of beautiful golden sand. The sea was warm and not unlike a millpond. There was a surprising number of Italian civilians enjoying a day at the beach. Alex and I went back the same way but called at a NAAFI bearing the name 'The Old Monastery' for a cup of tea and a wad.

I had a late dinner prepared by the tank crew and soon afterwards was very surprised at the arrival of a small echelon of store lorries and fitters. Sure enough our lorry was amongst them and so I was soon talking to George, Jock and Jack. I learnt that they had been ordered to come up because of modifications required to be carried out on the new tanks. The order came too late to prevent me travelling up as I did. George was full of comments about the beauty of their trip up over the Apennines, which took them most of the day. I helped to erect the sham-e-ola and moved in with them.

On 10 August we were all placed on a two-hour 'stand by', meaning we could move at any time but would only get two hours' notice of same. The weather was very hot now so Alex and I went for a quick swim in the afternoon. The day passed without any sign of the promised tanks turning up so the fitters and indeed most of us had an easy time. The next two days were spent in exactly the same manner with no sign of the new tanks.

The evening of 12 August however, brought new orders. The next morning we were to move off in Squadrons with the tanks moving on their tracks. At 03:00 on 13 August C Squadron tanks pulled out and we brought up the rear in our lorry, all following the road north in the wake of HQ, A and B Squadrons. There was a journey of nearly 100 miles to do but this was to take three days of very early morning moves in order to keep the highway clear for other forward supplies during daylight hours.

The tracked vehicles made quite good speed and their rumbling noise caused some locals in the villages and small towns to come out. At normal breakfast time we passed through the large seaside town of Pescara with women folk throwing bunches of roses at the tank crews. We even received one such bunch, which we fixed to the nose of our truck.

Soon after, at a place called Roseto, we all leaguered up near the sea and supplies of petrol came for refuelling. We had covered 37 miles well before the 09:00 deadline and, being self-contained now, cooked our breakfast. Our party went to bed for the afternoon and enjoyed a swim in the evening.

At 02:30 hours next morning I made a pot of porridge to put our party right for the road. We saw HQ, A and B Squadrons on their way but, before we moved, a dispatch rider arrived on the scene. It transpired we (C Squadron fitters and technical storemen) were to stay at that spot together with four tanks of the Squadron. Four tanks from each of A and B Squadrons would also be halted on the road and sent back. 12 new tanks were reckoned to have reached Ortona and would be sent on up to us. After this sudden piece of unexpected information had sunk in we returned to bed.

We got up for the second time on 14 August at about 08:30 to discover the four tanks each from A and B had indeed returned. This group stayed put until mid-afternoon when another dispatch arrived and this was an order for the 12 tanks and us to return to Ortona. We retraced yesterday's steps and reached Ortona in late evening, parking-up on the familiar spot.

I slept that night as a guest of Alex in his bivvy, as the original small advance party to Ortona was still there. Indeed, at that time, the Regiment was spread all over Italy. Some tanks were in Ortona along with a small number of trucks. The large tank group was on the way north and a small advance party with vehicles was at the northern grouping area. Then, of course, the main body of echelons was still down near Caserta. Goodness knows where Charlie, 'Nix' and Frank were, for I last saw them with the Carrier at Caserta railhead.

The next day following our return to Ortona, the expected new tanks failed to reach us so Alex and I enjoyed another afternoon on the beach with the occasional dip in the warm, calm water.

The following early morning, however, the original Ortona advance party, including Alex, moved off for the assembly point up north. This was on 16 August and at mid-day the new tanks turned up. Charlie, 'Nix' and Frank turned up too but they were without the Carrier. It seemed that after waiting several days at Caserta railhead, and after having the Regiment's six Carriers loaded on rail flats, orders were changed. This meant the dumping of these Carriers, just what everyone concerned had hoped for. After running them to an Ordnance Department near Naples the whole party had come up by train. Of course, Charlie and Co had loads of stores on the Carrier and this they had to struggle along with as best they could. In the words of Charlie, "'Twas a b... game carrying the stuff in relays from one point to another".

Now our party was together once more and while some slept under the sham-e-ola, George and I erected our bivvies joined together and shared the bigger tent. This day proved an extremely busy one for me. In fact the whole group at Ortona was busy for a further six days before modifications and other work was completed and recorded.

The group then moved to the assembly point some 100 miles further north travelling by way of the coast road. Near Civitanova, under cover of woodland, the whole Regiment was gathered. In fact, the complete 1st Armoured Division was in and around the area. We had an easy time for several days with occasional bathing allowed in the sea at Civitanova. I recall taking out a new type of paddleboat with Len Goring which we nearly turned over when we were quite a way out from land. In this area care was taken to camouflage and the mosquito net used in my bivvy also served to ward off those ever-tormenting flies.

One day we were all lectured about the forthcoming attack on the Gothic Line and, in particular, the plan for our Armoured Division. The plan was to hold us back until a way through the Line had been won when our armour was to break through to the north and move quickly through the Valley of the Po and race on to the Alps. However, things did not work out as planned.

Near the end of August rations were issued which once again made each vehicle self-contained for meals. Frank overhauled our party's two little pressure cookers; one, a primus type which had served us well since desert days and the other one we were presently using, which was an Italian brand. Mind you, we were always better placed than most, since I had several in store and spare parts too though I always made sure each tank was properly fixed up despite their misgivings about using their cookers.

CHAPTER TWENTY-TWO

MOVING NORTH

August to November 1944

At last light on the last day of August the Regiment's tanks, 63 in number, moved up forward to a staging area near Senigállia and were followed by the A Echelon's 'Flying Fitters' and supplies. The further approach march of the tanks during the following night proved hard and tiring and the advance during the night of 3 September in very wet conditions proved even more difficult than the previous night. The fording of Rivers Foglia and Conca proved hazardous, to say nothing of the enemy action.

There was no easy breakthrough. The Savino Ridge caused a hold-up for some while. We of B Echelon moved up a few miles early in September. On 5 September it took us four hours to do a further move forward of about eight miles. The heavy rain had made conditions slippery for wheeled vehicles and we ended up in a vineyard with loads of grapes at hand, only needing to be picked.

As at all times like this we remained on stand-by to move. This was a day when mail was received from home and it raised my spirits to hear that Arthur had been given leave to travel across India to see young Raymond who was suffering from malaria in Burma – both were my wife's brothers.

Mid-September saw us move a little further forward and for a while the weather improved, though conditions underfoot were still muddy. George and I were sharing a bivvy at this time and it became something like a Mosque insofar as we removed boots before entering because of the mud. We were able to watch from a ridge the large-scale activities of our bombers over enemy lines.

One day there was a cooking experiment by Charlie of our party so that we had the first of quite a few roly-poly duffs for dessert. These were made in one of Charlie's old vests. We used to tease him saying, "Is the vest clean or is it because you want it washed?" Despite our comments, we enjoyed the change of menu.

It may be worth a mention that our party had a loose routine with regard to preparing meals. As I was always up bright and early I did breakfast. Not having much to do at other times I spent spare half-hours writing letters and often did this in the bivvy. Just as in the mornings I used to shout, "Show a leg" to get them up for breakfast, so they would often shout to me at meal times, "Where's yer mess tin?" and "Where's yer mug?" or again, "For Lord's sake give over writing and come out of that flea-pit!".

During the latter half of September we had several short moves forward. The weather had again deteriorated with considerable rain and very cold winds and the mud had become glue-like. However, we were still sleeping in bivvies, save for an odd night or two spent in the lorry. We cut ditches around our bivvies and managed to keep surprisingly dry.

One day I had to travel out on duty a few miles so went as mate with a driver in a 15 cwt Bedford truck with chains on the rear wheels and we got on reasonably well. On the trip we saw some lorries being towed by teams of oxen from leaguering spots on to the road. Another day our echelon rations for four days arrived as far as a narrow road 300 yards away so all hands were needed to go and get them. We ended up carrying the bread in a blanket with one person on each corner.

It was about now that the Regiment's kit bags reached us from a store down south where they had been since June. We were thankful to have battledress uniforms again since the weather was now getting cold for K drill.

By the end of September we had moved just short distances a couple of times with the weather still being mainly indifferent. With regard to the Gothic Line attack, the end of the month saw our forward troops break through into the extensive Po Valley (or, more correctly, the Lombardy Plain) and out of the mountains and hills that had been so hard to gain.

October dawned with the break-up of the 1ˢᵗ Armoured Division but we still remained part of the 2ⁿᵈ Armoured Brigade, being attached to various Infantry Divisions in future. The Regiment also acquired a couple of Sherman Tanks with 105mm guns, one of which was allocated to C Squadron.

The first day of October brought a move forward of 12 miles by the rear echelon of ours and it was a bit dodgy getting into our latest leaguering area. Our party put away a quick dinner of warmed-up stew from tins, as it was one of those very rare nights when we were called on to do guard duty. I was NCO, with George, Jock and Jack doing the two hours on and four off. These sort of duties were 'a piece of cake' really in that there was no cleaning up for them to do and no proper guard-mounting parade.

The morning of 2 October dawned with drizzly rain after this rare duty of ours and it continued to rain all day. Nothing and nobody moved, except that Alex arrived on the scene with his little Bedford truck after having been away with an officer for some days.

We all now forsook our bivvies in favour of sleeping in the lorries. Charlie, Jock, George and Frank made themselves cosy in the back of the store lorry while Jack favoured the cab. I was offered, and accepted, a perfectly dry berth in the back of the 15 cwt Bedford along with Alex. Alex was still using my homemade bed which he had offered to transport for me from when we left St Marguerite. The rest of our party still transported their homemade ones in our rather crowded lorry but did not use them for bivvy sleeping, or when our lorry remained loaded and we were on stand-by to move.

Alex and I shared the Bedford truck for a few nights until he once again had to move. Fortunately this day proved a smashing one with warm sunshine, like a return to summer. Everything we had was put out to dry or air and we also aired ourselves by wearing only shorts. I heated up some water to give myself a good wash down. Of course I had to return to the old bivvy but managed to obtain some straw to lay down first. I guess it came from a nearby farm.

A day or so later a mobile canteen came to our spot so we were able to purchase a few goodies such as chocolate (from the old firm), fags, razor blades, soap and a few tins of fruit. It seemed left to chance as to when such a mobile canteen might turn up but when one did it was a most welcome event.

During the start of the second week in October our echelon moved forward down on to the plain but the ground there was so soft that after a few days we moved back several miles into the hills again. We all had to help in pushing our vehicles out of the leaguering place down there and one could only see the funny side with 20 'boys' trying to get round a lorry in order to push it free. The harder one shoved, the bigger the clods of mud on the boots.

On 23 October we moved yet again and once more down to the plain. The town of Cesena had by then been taken and our Regiment had been withdrawn from the push forward for a while, so the move by our echelon was to an area where our whole Squadron was together. Although being together for the first time in over two months, we were in fact spread over quite a large area because we were all at scattered farms, houses and outbuildings. Our party and the 'Flying Fitters' could be found at a farm where we had taken over three upstairs rooms reached by an outside flight of stone steps. Here we were very comfortable indeed with a large table for our meals and other civilised facilities that we had lacked for three years.

After a day or so we all had two inoculations in the left arm which made the arm very stiff for a time. It also left us with flu-like colds complete with the shivers.

Next day was to be a free day and our party stayed mostly in bed save for preparing and eating meals. The 'Clerk of Weather' must have known, since it never stopped raining for the whole day. This caused some flooding in the area and the road near the farm was like a stream. The Italian family living on the ground floor told us that snow, when it came, could be two or three feet deep. This family did some washing of dirty clothes for us and, as they would not take any money, we gave them some bread together with a few other small things, as we seemed to have plenty to offer at the time.

The stay here was for a couple of weeks but less for the tank crews. It is worth a mention that George and Jock had left our party to take over a Tank Recovery Tank, which was a tank-like vehicle capable of towing or hoisting tanks from ditches, streams, rivers, canals and bogs, which abounded on that great Northern Plain particularly in wintertime. It meant they would have to operate up close to the tanks. Another experiment by the Regiment was to form a small troop of three vehicles called Bridging Tanks. They were specially adapted tanks carrying Bailey bridging parts.

B Echelon, including us, moved from this area early in November and ended up some 18 miles further north. During this move our party spent one night on a roadside because one of our lorries had broken down. We found the echelon leaguering spot the next morning and soon found ourselves a house for a billet. It was in the countryside and was owned by a young married couple with one small son.

The husband was a builder by trade and at the time was

repairing war damage to his own home. Our reduced party, of now only Charlie, Frank, Jack and I, used a large upstairs room. While we were here the weather improved a great deal and we had many days of sunshine. By 17:30 it became dark and the temperature dropped so we all welcomed the invitation to spend evenings in the family's living room all seated around a big log fire. Somewhere the electric power had been put out of order so there was only a large oil lamp placed on the table. This situation lasted about 12 days when we were again on the move forward.

This move saw us billeted at a huge farmhouse where we took over a large upstairs room. The place had been knocked about somewhat and some of the rooms had big shell holes in the outer walls. Our room had no fireplace but we were otherwise OK since Charlie managed to fix up a small light from a battery and also got the little wireless set going again. We would retire to bed very early to keep warm, sometimes reading or perhaps sitting up in bed with a couple of woollies on if doing a spot of writing.

We were still doing well for ourselves in the food line and were cooking some smashing dinners, particularly as local produce was used to supplement our daily rations. We sometimes compared these with the dinners of our earlier desert days when the choice was bully beef and biscuits or stew.

For us there was hardly any kind of work to be done except keeping the lorry ship-shape and ourselves well fed and warm. Things at this time must have been much more difficult for the tanks and forward echelon supply vehicles.

CHAPTER TWENTY-THREE

FORLI

November 1944 to January 1945

A Cold Christmas

The last week of November brought yet another move in drizzly rain. It was a move of only eight miles but it was of interest since we passed through the fair-sized town of Forli, the birthplace of Mussolini. We saw no Italian civilians in the streets. Maybe the rain had kept them in or they had fled the town.

Having driven about a mile north of Forli and crossed the perfectly intact bridge over the river we turned left into a side lane where, soon, numerous tracks led us to a scattering of farms. We ended up at a typical small farm where, unfortunately, there was no space for us in the house. However, an adjoining outbuilding with large double doors was perfectly acceptable as a billet. We soon took over and moved in, complete with our cooking utensils. The drizzly rain lasted for 36 hours so outside the ground became a quagmire.

Duty took us up to the tanks the next afternoon for a brief while and we found them out of action and resting for a few days. The driver of the truck and I had only just started the return trip in the last of the daylight when Ack-Ack gunfire started. We stopped the truck and bailed out, away from the edge of the road. It was a very rare appearance of the Luftwaffe. The aircraft dropped their bombs and disappeared as quickly as they came. The first words of our party when I walked in was, "How did you get on with the fireworks?" and I was able to reply, "Nothing happened near us".

December was now upon us and by this time we were being invited in with the family during the evenings. They had a large open grate with a big log fire. During this first week in December most of us wrote and sent off our Christmas mail. My lettercard to my wife and young son had a small drawing at the heading. The drawing was of a flying dove carrying in its beak a sprig of holly and a message on a card reading "CHRISTMAS GREETINGS 1944".

Still being in the same place in the middle of the month, we had decided to rig up a fire stove in the outbuilding. It was made from an old metal ammunition box and was suitable for burning wood and small logs.

I was still cooking breakfast as my share of preparing meals for our party and, indeed, was always first up in the morning. At this time no-one of our party was up before 09:00 hours and quite often it was closer to 10:00. I think Jack held the record with 16 hours in bed!

About this time the town of Faenza was taken but, in general, both forces were gradually preparing to hold their positions for the winter though there were still occasional bursts of activity. Even in our quarters we would sometimes hear the whine of shells travelling through the air.

We were still sometimes joining the family in the big farm kitchen with the huge log fire. Always, right in the corner of the fireplace sat the farmer's youngest son, Salvano. He used to spend a great deal of the daytime with us. He was eight years old and never used to talk much, probably because of the language problems; however, he certainly used to like our chocolate and sweets.

One evening I was involved in a laughable incident. They had a water pipe over the sizeable kitchen sink but the water had to be pumped from a pump situated just outside the door in the open yard. The mother required water for some reason so I, being seated nearest the door, offered to go out and operate the pump. Presently there was a shout of "Basta! Basta!" and I assumed she wanted me to pump faster so, of course, I obliged. There was water going all over the place until someone pulled me away and Frank, our brainy one, explained that 'basta' in Italian means 'enough'. I had to apologise as the mother received a good drenching!

With only a few days to go before 25 December we heard that C Squadron tanks would remain in the Line over Christmas but HQ, B and A Squadrons would return to Forli for the two days, after which A Squadron would relieve C Squadron. The echelons of B Squadron personnel were to have Christmas dinner at a large farmhouse central to our leaguering area.

Since August, however poor the weather had been, the Squadron Quartermaster had delivered food rations to all Squadron vehicles wherever they were leaguered. The usual practice was to expect him every third day. Tank crews may not have received deliveries quite so regularly but they always had emergency rations in reserve. The Squadron Quartermaster and his staff were based in our echelon and it was he who made the arrangement for the farmhouse, that was central to us all, to be available for the 25th. For that day, too, the Squadron cooks would do the catering.

On 23 December snow fell for most of the day and continued overnight so we awoke on Christmas Eve to discover a thick mantle over everything. That day was a very cold one. There was a bitter wind blowing from the north so we didn't move far from our fire all day.

Christmas morning saw us up bright and early and I melted down a pot of snow for washing and shaving. Breakfast was being served at the farmhouse from 08:30 to 09:00 so we drove the lorry over. While devouring porridge, bacon and sausages, etc, we heard that a load of mail had come up late the previous evening. True enough, most had a welcome letter or two from home. It was a surprise to see Alex at breakfast too. He had come back from the forward echelon on Christmas Eve so I invited him over to our farm later in the morning.

At about 11:00 Alex came over as arranged and we both went for a long brisk walk in the snow. Overhead it was a perfect blue sky and the sunshine was brilliant. Despite the War Front being so near there was beauty to be seen everywhere, for the trees and evergreen bushes painted a pretty picture. Every leaf was lined with a white snowy icicle and one felt they only needed coloured lights to make them become Christmas trees. There was also a very common tree with long hanging grass-like leaves, which looked just lovely.

Our Christmas dinner was to be at 13:00 and all were assembled in good time. A long table was laid the length of the big farmhouse room and the seating was on forms. WD maps laid face down served as tablecloths and there were bunches of evergreens about the walls. About 26 of us were seated for a really good meal of turkey, pork, potatoes, cauliflower and peas, followed by Christmas pudding, fruit and custard. There was also ample wine available but there was only one toast, "Good luck to our tank crews". Afterwards, free goodies were passed down the table, these being blocks of chocolate, packets of sweets, blocks of soap, PK chewing gum, razor blades and a few oranges. There was a short impromptu concert which did not last long and, as the party broke up, each man was issued with two bottles of beer.

I went back to Alex's farm billet for a time but got back to our place before dusk. Our party had been invited to the farm for an evening dinner with the family but, just at the time for us to go in, Jerry 'planes came over. There was considerable gunfire and the sky was filled with the colour traces of Ack-Ack. We guessed that bombs had been directed at Faenza.

The Christmas evening with the farm family was a great success. Seated for the dinner were 12 of them and six of us. It started with a kind of macaroni and soup and then it was roast turkey alone, then roast rabbit with vegetables. The meal ended with a kind of cake dish and there was, of course, the normal Italian wine. After the meal we all sat in an arc round the roaring log fire and gave the youngsters some of our goodies. Later on Charlie fetched the wireless in and the family were pleased about that. We retired to our beds very near midnight. Some of us were up at about 10:00 the next morning, only to discover that everything had frozen up.

On 27 December we heard that the switch of A Squadron and C Squadron tanks in the Line had taken place and our Squadron had taken over the billets of A Squadron in Forli. On the 28th we, Technical Stores and Fitters, were ordered to join with the rest of Technical Stores and Fitters of the Regiment in Forli. The others had moved to Forli several days before and formed a group together working on the tanks and support vehicles. We said goodbye to the friendly farm people where we had been comfortably billeted for almost five weeks.

The Eastern Coast

I had some tank spares known to be required by the 'Flying Fitters' so, instead of driving directly to where the technical group were, we first sought out our Technical Sergeant 'Blondy' Osborne. We found him at a hall in Forli where the tank crews and forward echelon people were having their Christmas dinner. We heard from him that the tank group were to be on 'stand by' again as from that night. As there was much work to be done we were advised to stay by the tanks and he told us he would find some billets for us later on. With our lorry standing at the roadside our fitters got busy at once and were joined by the 'Flying Fitters' team once the meal was over and they had changed from battle dress into overalls. It was 21:00 when we settled in the room of a small house and had a wood fire burning.

On the last day of the year C Squadron tanks were still in Forli. It had been a busy few days for our party but the work was now complete.

The town of Forli was quite large but driving was a bit of a problem because all the main roads were one way only. The traffic at this time was service vehicles only and to ride anywhere could involve a detour around the circuit.

1 January 1945 brought about the move of the tanks and forward echelon back up into the Line again. Although there was no great initiative by either side, a Line had to be held as there was action now and again such as an attack on some farmhouse thought to be a billet or observation post. In one such affair Sergeant Ross, Commanding a C Squadron Tank Troop, won the Military Medal.

On the afternoon of this New Year's Day, 'Nix' and I walked into town and after the customary 'shay² and wad' went to an ENSA variety show presented by a South African Concert Party. The theatre was packed with troops.

Near our billets at Forli were baths and it was a real treat during our stay to be able to have a number of hot showers. A good thing too was that, at a particular desk, one could hand in dirty underwear and socks and receive back all new clothes in exchange.

The weather stayed cold but the snow had melted, although it could still be seen on the distant hills. However, at the end of the first week of the New Year snow fell for a complete period of 24 hours. In Forli the roads were soon cleared to aid the movement of military traffic but otherwise it was lying some nine inches deep. As the weather stayed freezing cold, this snow remained a long time and walking about was very tricky. A South African

Unit near our billet made two large snow statues, one each side of their entrance gate. These stayed intact for days. It was a time of red noses and handkerchiefs but we managed to get warm indoors. As at home, I usually had a seat next to the fire. The wood would be piled on and my mates would then pull my leg when I was forced to draw back. When we did go outside for duty or pleasure it seemed strange to be wearing overcoats, gloves and scarves.

One day around this time I had to go forward a few miles to Faenza on a brief duty and found Highway 9 cleared of snow. Another time out was when Len Goring of Technical HQ Stores and I went into town to see a film called 'This Heavenly Body' featuring Hedy Lamour and William Powell. It was a silly picture really but had some humour in it.

By mid-January news that the Regiment was due to pull out and move back some miles became known. On the 17th our echelon was all loaded up ready for the move but it was cancelled at the last minute. We think the icy state of the roads and volume of traffic were the reasons. 'Nix' and I decided on a walk into town that afternoon to visit the NAAFI, or to use its posh name, 'The Dorchester Club'. For a change we went in to the restaurant instead of the popular snack bar. We had not been there long enough to place our order, when in walked George and Jock. We had not seen them since they had taken over the Recovery Tank so at a table for four we ate, drank (tea) and talked away for nearly two hours. George and Jock told us they had been so busy up front with their Recovery Tank that no break had been possible and they were two of the very few in the Regiment who had not been drawn back for the Christmas dinner. It seemed that they had a very rough Christmas Day and Boxing Day for George said, "I'll never forget this Christmas as long as I live". All they had to eat on the 25th was one bacon sandwich!

They were in Forli now because a convoy of tank transporters carrying the Regiment's vehicles south had been halted in the town during the previous night and had still not been allowed to proceed further south. Although George and Jock were travelling down with them, their Recovery Tank was not, because it had hit a mine a few days before withdrawal.

Footnotes

[2] Shay (sometimes spelt shai or chai) may have derived from Arabic chai, cockney char, or from the original Chinese Ch'a, all meaning tea.

CHAPTER TWENTY-FOUR

PESARO TO THE APENNINES

January to March 1945

Pesaro

By 20 January the whole of the Regiment had withdrawn a good many miles to the south of Forli and were billeted in large empty houses ranged along the seafront at Pesaro. It would have been great had it been summertime, although there hadn't been any snow there and it was particularly pleasant to see green fields again.

A large vacant open space along one end of Pesaro seafront was where all the Squadron tanks parked up, in Squadron line, with the wheeled vehicles parked in a similar fashion nearby. Over the course of the next few days, two big leave parties left the Regiment involving three-quarters of the personnel. One group went to Florence followed the next day by a smaller group to Rome. All of our party went off except for 'Nix' and me.

That week in Pesaro was a busy one for me right from the time of arrival, for lots of checking of the tanks had to be done. Also, five new lorries were taken over which meant more checking and detail to be returned to the Technical HQ Office. In addition, I was the recipient of a new Technical Store Lorry that was fitted out with new metal bins and other equipment. The transfer of stores and the personal kit of our party, which included mine, had to be completed with most of the 'boys' from our party away. After the rush and bustle of daylight hours it was a treat to have a quiet evening with 'Nix' and me reading, writing or simply making toast by the fire.

For some weeks past Sergeant Bennett of Technical HQ had been away in hospital with an illness. His absence gave rise to speculation of promotions and these appeared in Orders during this period at Pesaro. 'Dolly' Dolton, the B Squadron Technical Storeman, was promoted from Corporal to Sergeant, I from Lance Corporal to Corporal and Len Goring from Trooper to Lance Corporal. 'Dolly' moved to HQ, Len Goring to B Squadron, leaving me still in C Squadron. I was glad of that.

The leave party from Florence returned on time after their seven days' leave but the Rome party's leave was cut short by two days as they were recalled under orders. They arrived back at 04.00 hours after a 16-hour train journey. Charlie thought Florence was a beautiful city but the road trip back over the icy mountain roads had been a nightmare.

The reason for the sudden flap was that the Regiment was being recalled to the Front Line but would go as Infantry. There was only a day or two for preparation and things were a bit hectic. Personal arms were to be taken and it was decided to take all the small arms and machine guns from the tanks, nearly all of which would remain at Pesaro. The fitters were busy dismounting these guns while we technical storemen were trying to sort out who would be responsible for each gun and obtaining signatures for same. Some wheeled vehicles were taken as troop transporters and George, Jock and

Alex went as drivers, amongst others of course. 'Nix' and I, who had kept fingers crossed for a week hoping for a third leave party decided 'we'd had it'.

The personnel of the Regiment who stayed put at Pesaro included fitters, some driver mechanics, electricians and Squadron technical storemen, together with the LAD. The Squadron's 'Flying Fitters' went up north as also did the Technical Office, presumably because a number of wheeled vehicles would remain based there.

LAD had their own little area of billets but most of the others moved into two medium sized hotels right near the beach and adjacent to the large vehicle park. There was also another small group, as there were two of each of the four Squadron's Quartermasters, stores and cooks' lorries and staff. I now found myself sharing a nice comfortable room with three other technical storemen – Len Goring of B, Corporal Williams of A and Corporal Bates of HQ. Others of our party who stayed were Charlie, 'Nix' and Frank but they were in billets with other technical people respectively.

All the vehicles remaining in Pesaro were to undergo a complete check so there was some work to be done. Also everyone would share guard duties.

In our hotel room we had a window which looked out over the beach and sea and it also had a flat roof suitable for sunbathing if – that little word 'if' – it had been summertime. As it was, Corporal Bates provided a lovely fire stove, one he had been carrying around from billet to billet. This stove was rather large for our room and needed a good supply of wood to keep it going but that was easy to come by. 'Sticky' (Corporal Bates) and I used a big crosscut saw from one of our store lorries for cutting branches of trees or sometimes small trunks.

In Pesaro there were a couple of service clubs, one a NAAFI and one a YMCA, which were used from time to time, usually for the customary tea and wad. A hall in the town was taken over by a mobile cinema unit so picture shows were available, though only with a small screen. The first picture I saw there was in the company of Len Goring and was called 'Madame Curie', a picture that depicted the discovery of radium.

This first week in February brought news from home about the destruction by fire of The Colston Hall, Bristol but not through any enemy action. 'It will be a great loss', the newspaper cutting said.

Some of the days here began to brighten up so it was nice for a group of us to walk along the beach towards the headland. Guard duty at this time was not really a hardship as there was no 'spit and polish' or formal guard drill. The loss of sleep could generally be made up if needed. Len Goring and I attended another picture show. The film was called 'The Iron Road' and was about the railroads ousting the covered wagons from the Wild West. It was a lousy picture – perhaps ENSA had been showing it in the 1914 War. There was a girl, a hero and a villain in the story so the 'boys' took the show in hand by cheering the hero, hissing the villain and so on, thus creating their own fun.

Early on Sunday 18 February Len Goring and I departed with a lorry from Pesaro to make the trip up to where our technical office and echelon of vehicles were leaguered in Ravenna. Our job here was to hand back

18 of the Regiment's oldest wheeled vehicles and to take over 18 new ones. We reached our technical office by early afternoon and, after discussion with Technical Quartermaster Dobbins, learnt that the take over would not be until the next day.

Len and I then had a wander round Ravenna for a few hours. We called in at a club called 'Eric's Nook' where a good Italian trio entertained the troops and they received our support for an hour. Ravenna, we found, wasn't nearly as large a town as Forli and there was little there for the troops. Of course, the winter Front Line was only a few miles north of there.

The technical personnel had a busy Monday morning but the job was completed by 15:00 hours so Len and I set off on the return trip to Pesaro. We decided not to travel right back that day although we could easily have done so. Instead we called at a farm up in the hills, some way off the normal route, where we had previously spent some time. We were warmly greeted by the farm family and spent a jolly evening with the aid of a gramophone. We slept that night in a civvy bed, complete with sheets and did not rise too early next morning. After a breakfast of fried eggs and finding the morning to be a glorious one with blue sky and sunshine, we went for a walk of several miles down through a valley. We returned to the farm for lunch about mid-day and there was much laughter over our efforts to fork-up spaghetti!

On the lorry we were carrying a heavy sack of mail back to Pesaro, so on reaching there we sorted this out and I was lucky to have a number of items, including several letters, a parcel and a bundle of Bristol Evening Posts.

At the end of that week on Saturday 24 February, a party set off in a lorry for Rimini about 20 miles up the coast. George, 'Nix' and I were in the group in the back of the lorry. The event that attracted us was a soccer match between the 8th Army and the RAF. This was quite a big match as wartime football went and was a return game to the drawn 1-1 match that had been played on Boxing Day which we had not seen. Rimini Stadium was full for some time before the start – two grandstands, terracing and several rows deep standing around the touchline. The Southern Highlanders Pipe Band played while marching up and down. Most of the players taking part had been with professional clubs back home, the 8th Army's Captain being Andy Beattie. It was a splendid match which must have impressed the few thousand Italians who mingled with the crowd. The 8th Army XI won by 2 goals to 1. The convoy of Army and all services transport leaving afterwards must have been the largest seen by the townspeople. The star of the 8th Army XI was the outside right Tom Finney (Preston N E) who, as reported earlier, was in our Brigade with the Queen's Boys.

During the last week of the month the weather was really fine with plenty of sunshine and the temperature picking up. On the Sunday five of us, including George, went to a rare evening service in the Church of England tradition held at a Church in the town. Afterwards we bundled into the YMCA canteen and laden with a hymn book and shay and wad, joined the 20:00 community hymn singing. With about 120 people all seated at small tables the singing went well and though advertised to last half an hour, it was after 21:00 when we departed. Everyone stood for the last hymn which was 'The day Thou gavest Lord is ended'.

On 26 February Len Goring and I travelled in a truck to a town called Iesi, some 45-50 miles further south. Our journey was to return surplus stores to an Ordnance Depot. We went via the coast road to Ancona and then turned inland to reach our destination. We had lunch at a South African Club in Iesi before making the return trip.

We returned just in time for our evening dinner and while eating who should 'blow in' but Alex. He and I talked for a long while and it was a treat to see him on his birthday. He had driven down in the 15cwt Bedford from Ravenna and had as his passenger Captain Bryant. They were making a few hours' stop for a break and meal before travelling on all night to Rome which they hoped to reach by 08:00 the next morning. Captain Bryant was going down on seven days' leave and Alex was to remain there too. As a point of interest, Captain Bryant of C Squadron hailed from Cribbs Causeway, Bristol and I passed on to him many bundles of Evening Post newspapers which had been sent to me, especially so during the Western Desert days when he was a Lieutenant.

Another film show came to Pesaro in early March and Len Goring and I went along one evening to see 'In Which We Serve' and enjoyed it. Also, we did another trip down to Iesi. There were now signs of another imminent move!

Rimini, Forli, Ravenna and the Apennines
One day the tank drivers came back to Pesaro and next day the tanks were loaded on to transporters. The tanks, together with the convoy, again moved north. The Pesaro

group, which once again saw our party together on the store lorry, moved up on 7 March.

This move ended in an area between Forli and Ravenna where the Regiment were together but billeted in scattered farms over a large area. The 'Flying Fitters' and we were in a farmhouse together and, being self-contained, we mucked in together preparing meals. We shared a big downstairs room complete with a large fireplace and, of course, a fire. I was still up in the mornings before most of the (increased) party and was therefore still preparing breakfast.

It proved a busy time for most of the technical people, both for tradesmen and we storemen, so that we had a spell when our evening dinners got later and later. On his return from Rome, Alex would sometimes come over to chat for an hour or so.

About the middle of the month there was another big football game, this time in Ravenna and was between the 8th Army and the 5th Army. Our group did not attend. Unfortunately we were all too busy and could not spare the time.

By the last week of March the tanks were being used extensively for training exercises and were away for the majority of the time so we were able to take a break. In any case, our group's busy period was ending. On 29 March it appeared on Regimental Orders that I would be reverting to Lance Corporal. All those recent technical staff promotions were reverted because Sergeant Bennett came back to 10th Royal Hussars after his time in hospital. These promotions had been backdated to 28 December 1944 so we had to revert after 89 days because, had it been delayed one more day (90 days), we would have become War Substantiated and could not then have been reverted. Our Technical Officer interviewed me and explained that Squadron Technical Storemen should hold the rank of Corporal as was so in A, B and HQ, but HQ Squadron had two. He could, he stated, put Corporal Turner into C Squadron and switch me to HQ Squadron. I commented that I had been in C Squadron as a Lance Corporal for quite a time and would be more content to stay that way rather than to switch over.

On the morning of 30 March, Good Friday, I did the rounds of all vehicles in order to complete a weekly statement of mileages. This was routine, demanded by Technical HQ office when the Regiment was out of battle. Under such circumstances tank mileages, in particular, often had to be restricted. I was climbing out of a tank turret when I noticed our Squadron Sergeant Major ('Buck') Jones standing watching near by. He at once called me, shouting, "Lance Corporal Crocker, I want you" and I, jumping down from the tank, wondered why. On reaching him he said, "How would you like seven days' leave in Rome?" Of course, I replied that it would be nice, so he then said, "OK, you and Corporal Graham can go together. Be ready and report at the Squadron office truck tomorrow morning at 08:00". So, 'Nix' and I were going to have a period of leave after all.

The start of this leave had to be postponed for 24 hours and it was a little later than 08:00 on Easter Sunday when 'Nix' and I and three 'boys' from a tank troop were picked up by a truck from Brigade HQ. There were a few others to be picked up from elsewhere so eventually a group of about 18 were in the truck.

We were driven to Rimini railway station arriving at about 10:45 to find the station alive with troops all heading for leave. After about an hour all of us on the station were given a hot meal and later were called out in groups to board the train. It so happened that the 2nd Armoured Brigade was the first group called so we entrained in the end coach. We looked forward to travelling in a normal passenger train with corridors for a change.

The packed leave train steamed out of Rimini at 13:00 and into platform 22 in Rome at spot on 06:00 the next morning, Easter Monday, 2 April. There was one stop en-route where a hot meal and tea was served. Also at this stop any watches and clocks were put forward one hour. Most managed to have a little doze or light sleep during the night but I was awake in the early hours and, by the light of the moon, watched from the corridor as our train chuffed through the Apennines.

CHAPTER TWENTY-FIVE

ROME & RIMINI

April to May 1945

On Leave in Rome

Transport met us at Rome station and conveyed us to a very large building on the city's outskirts that was run on Rest Camp lines. Army vehicles were being run like a shuttle 'bus service to and from the centre of Rome. 'Nix' and I soon discovered one or two things. First of all, Rome was now a much more normal city than when we were last there some nine months before. There were not so many servicemen about and the street lighting, buses, tramcars, private cars and shops made it look far more like a peacetime city. Secondly, we found that quite a number of the troops on leave did not use the Army facilities on the outskirts all of the time. It was rather commonplace for them to rent a flat in town.

On 3 April 'Nix' and I took over a flat in Rome for four nights. It was just being vacated by two other servicemen on leave and so was recommended. It meant we would not be obliged to travel to and from the city outskirts and also provided a change from the Army atmosphere. It did also mean we would have to buy all required meals in the city but we would have done so for most meals in any case. There were numerous service clubs available as well as some Italian restaurants, so this was no trouble at all.

A regular occurrence in the central part of the city was to be confronted by Italians taking quick snapshots with tiny cameras. One would then be presented with a card stating that the photo would be ready in 24 hours for a small charge at such and such an address. I had this done a number of times but only ever collected two lots. I did however have a photo taken in a studio shop as well. All these were sent home in due course and were much appreciated. There was a special reason for having the studio photo done because it was taken on 4 April, being the date of my son Colin's 6th birthday.

'Nix' had made friends with a family in Rome some nine months before when the Regiment was stationed in the area; therefore he very often spent a day, or part of a day, with them. I did not mind this since there were things I also wanted to do.

On the afternoon of the 4th I went to seek out Norman Anderson, who I knew to be still stationed at No. 104 Hospital. Norman, a civilian friend, and I used to keep in touch by letter, since both of us were in the same war area and there was always a possibility we might meet. Our only other meeting had been about 11 months' ago near Naples, shortly after my arrival in Italy.

Well, there was no trouble at all in finding the No. 104 Hospital as it was very central and quite near the ancient Colosseum. There was great pleasure attached to such a meeting and I'm sure we both felt that as we chatted away. Norman was looking very well indeed and was most chirpy over the war situation in general. I was able to add that a spring offensive had started up north or, if not, would be starting any time soon. I mentioned that it was Colin's birthday and Norman provided a real birthday tea for me at the Hospital. We later went to the Argentine Theatre where we saw the play 'The Late Christopher Bean' which was once performed at our church hall at home. After the show we made arrangements to meet on Friday the 6th and would go, if possible, to the Rome Opera House.

The main servicemen's club in the city was called the Alexander Club and this huge place was situated in Via Venti Settembre. The Club was thoroughly up-to-date in every way. It provided exceptional opportunities for both rest and entertainment of every kind for all men of the Allied Forces. For good reason it had been called the finest club in the world. A real treat that I fully enjoyed on this leave was to have at least three hot baths at the Alexander Club, where 'Nix' and I used to have breakfast.

'Nix' and I had the day together on the 5 April and in the morning, on the sixth floor of the club, saw the film 'Laurie' which was both free and particularly entertaining. Most of our afternoon was spent in some beautiful hillside gardens named Villa Borghese Park. From here there were wonderful views over the city with all the prominent buildings being easy to pinpoint. We had both visited most of these buildings on previous periods of leave so gave them a miss this time.

A couple of times during the week we bumped into the three C Squadron tank 'boys' who travelled down with us. This usually ended by going into a wine bar for a glass of 'vino' and a chat. Photos and snaps we had all recently had taken were shown around and, for a while, we were all in a most happy mood together.

The time came around for me to once again link up with Norman Anderson and so, at the appointed hour, we met outside the great Opera House. Norman had one of his Army buddies with him and also announced that he had tickets for the show. The Opera House really was huge and we found ourselves at the back of the highest balcony. Nevertheless, it proved a splendid viewpoint for everything and also to appreciate the acoustics. The opera we saw was Othello with the lead part played and sung by Renato Gigli. Top people from the world of opera performed the other parts. The theatre was packed to capacity, mostly by Italian civilians but with a fair sprinkling of uniformed personnel. Between Acts and especially at the end of the performance the applause was terrific and there were prolonged shouts of "Bravo, bravo". The night was something always to be remembered by Norman and me.

We also linked up on the following night (Saturday) when, after a good chinwag over a tea and wad at a club, we again went to the Argentine Theatre. This time the Italian Police Force Band gave a concert of top class music that was most enjoyable. Afterwards we said goodbye to each other with a promise to write after a period of time. That night I returned to the Army Leave Centre on the outskirts and found 'Nix' already tucked up in bed, though we did manage a chat.

The next day, Sunday, we spent more leisurely, starting with a late breakfast and not going into town until late afternoon. We found the Leave Centre had every possible amenity for our comfort so that leave could be taken without even going into the city. The Centre comprised three buildings set amid grassland and gardens, each one being four storeys high. We understood it was to have been a school but now each block had been given the name of well-known London hotels – The Ritz, Dorchester and Savoy. 'Nix' and I were in the Savoy!

We were back from the centre of Rome early that evening and then learnt that our departure time the next day had been altered from mid-day to 17:00! We were able to spend most of another day in lazy fashion catching up on a spot of writing, something that was most welcome after all the activity during the week.

Our train steamed away from Rome station at about 18:00 on Monday 9 April.

Victory in Europe!

It was known by then that the Spring Offensive had started up north and we wondered how things were going.

Our train halted somewhere late that evening and we were served a couple of cheese sandwiches and a mug of tea. Eventually Rimini was reached at about 07:00 the next morning and everyone partook of a decent cooked breakfast. All of us from the 2nd Armoured Brigade were later picked up by a Brigade truck, the driver telling us that all Regiments had moved from where we had left them. This was what had been expected anyhow.

Forli was reached with a demand for a stop at the familiar Dorchester Club for a shay and wad. We travelled on in a northeasterly direction and eventually reached

Brigade HQ. We of the 10th Hussars were told to get some lunch while a message was sent out for a lorry of the Regiment to come and collect us. The group had a much longer wait than anticipated so the Brigade also had to provide dinner.

Our 10th Hussars truck turned up about 19:15 and, after a mostly bumpy and dusty drive, reached B echelon at nearly 20:00. Some of the group, including C Squadron's three tank crew, went off to report back to the officer of the echelon. 'Nix' and I walked over to rejoin our party in the store lorry. Seeing they all had bivouacs erected for sleeping, 'Nix' and I set about putting ours up. There was some mail awaiting our return and I read my good share in the bivvy by the light of a small torch. The following morning the 'boys' of our party reckoned it had been a very noisy night but I never heard a thing being so dead tired after practically no sleep the night before.

Later that morning we took our bivouacs down because of a Stand-to order to move and we did, in fact, move forward a couple of miles.

We did not move the next day 12 April and with little to do except wait, I caught up on some writing. Friends of mine from home, Harold and Cliff Baker, from whom I had received letters now and again, were in a Red Cross unit now in Europe. In a letter to them written that day I expressed the optimistic war news thus, 'The Sunbeams (Monty's Second Front Sunbeams) are causing all our hearts to wobble in delightful expectancy'. At quiet times like this I stayed in the bivouac for long periods writing letters for home and friends. Others seemed to dash off a letter in no time at all and, as usual, I had my leg pulled. Jack was frequently the one to peep inside the tent and remark, "Multi-scribe".

Between then and 20 April we had a number of short forward moves and Alex was now back in the echelon so we spent a lot of time together. I had not seen George and Jock since before my leave as they were still further forward with the Recovery Tank.

On 16 April I told Alex it was my Wedding Anniversary and I hoped that my wife (Hilda) would receive the flowers I had ordered through Interflora at Rome's Alexander Club.

One day during this period I had to do a trip out to collect a replacement part for a three-ton lorry damaged by a small mine. I had to take a truck and driver so chose Alex and his 15 cwt Bedford. We found the Mobile Ordnance near Ravenna and after I had obtained the replacement part we went into the town for a shay and wad. The funny thing was, that neither of us had a lira on us to pay but we had our shay and wad all right! In a hurry, we had both changed from shorts into battle dress. The weather had been dry and sunny so we were becoming salmon pink before the brown tan took over.

One of the recent short moves was during the night between 19:00 and 05:00 hours when we only managed to travel about five miles. Mostly we were stopped entirely, wedged in a huge traffic jam, due to it being only a single road passing through the countryside, which was also flooded.

The Regiment's area of battle was around Lake Comacchio and to advance, the Rivers Reno, Santerno and a maze of tributaries and irrigation canals had to be crossed. It was an area in which pontoon and Bailey bridges played an important role. Some of the canals ran at a higher level than the road due to high banking which in places had blown causing flooding. The night 20/21 April was a particularly noisy one with our heavy guns being active for long spells. We again had several short moves between then and 24 April.

The news coming from the other parts of Europe was also very encouraging. Alex, who had been good company during those past couple of weeks, went off on duty to take an officer down to Naples in the 15cwt Bedford truck. However, not all news was good. On the evening of the 24th we heard that C Squadron had, a few days before, lost several tanks. The crew of one of these had been killed. 'Nix' and I were shocked because Troopers Pateman and Hotchkiss of this crew were two of the tank 'boys' with us on the recent period of leave in Rome.

25 April saw the Regiment withdrawn from battle with other Units taking up the chase after the now fast re-treating enemy. During that morning our echelon moved forward, bypassing Ferrara, to within a few miles of the River Po's south bank. There, that same afternoon the whole Regiment concentrated around some farm buildings, not yet realising that the end of an arduous campaign had, for us, already arrived.

After 20 days in The Line it was great to relax, even for us in the rear echelon. Our party and the 'Flying Fitters' were leaguered in the area of a large farm but the weather was so good now that there was no need to use the farm buildings at all and most of us slept in our bivvies.

Charlie had our wireless working well and it was with much eagerness that we listened to the various news reports. It was on Wednesday 2 May that a News Flash created much excitement. It stated that Field Marshall Kesselring had, at Caserta, surrendered all the German Forces still in the Italian theatre of war to Field Marshall Alexander. So a once proud Army of 1,000,000 men had laid down their arms and all equipment. We could now thank God for that. For us it had been a very long slog from Alamein to the Alps but in the end every mile had been worthwhile. We all hoped that the next country we might find ourselves in would be 'Merry England'.

The 'boys' did some celebrating, firing small arms into the air. There was no wine available, at least not at our farm, but the Regiment made an issue of rum. During the evening the bells from a nearby church were ringing and I recall it affected me very much, perhaps because they conveyed something of the joy of those at home.

Only a few days after our jubilant experience of victory in Italy came the wonderful news of the German surrender in Europe. We heard over the air that a day of holiday with grand celebrations was to take place in England, and would be known as VE Day. This further victory by the Allied Forces left our party gathered round the Italian farm in a state of suspended animation. We wondered, 'Where do we go from here – home, or to suffer the slings of fortune in other places for a bit longer?'

It really was a most pleasant spot at the farm. The weather was spring-like, the sound of the cuckoo was often heard and this was the place where VE Day was spent. We had often wondered just where we might be when it came, so would never forget it.

From the point of view of actually celebrating though, it was rather low key and so our party spent this special day relaxing in lazy fashion. You can picture a party of seven or eight lazing on the grass, wearing only shorts in the blazing sunshine and listening on the wireless for hours on end to the great celebrations in London and many other parts of the British Isles. We heard Churchill and the King speak and listened to the packed masses in Whitehall, Trafalgar Square and outside Buckingham Palace, where the Royal Family appeared on the balcony. We were taken over to Cardiff and heard, too, the bells of Bath Abbey. Just how many times did we say, "Wish I was there"!

After dark we retired to the back of our store lorry and continued to listen in until midnight. There was hardly a word spoken by any of us. Nobody seemed to want to say much, which was just as well, as I think we all had large lumps in our throats. We felt grateful to commentators, such as Howard Marshall and others, who painted such vivid pictures of the scenes for us.

On 10 May the 8th Army held a Thanksgiving Service at a large theatre in Ferrara. All the 8th Army Regiments who were at that time in and around the area of Ferrara attended. There was no big parade or show or anything like that. The 10th Royal Hussars, I recall, were in the top balcony of the theatre and the service was very moving.

CHAPTER TWENTY-SIX

NORTHERN ITALY

May to June 1945

To Palmanova

The Regiment moved the following day. We once again had to rejoin the 56th Division, which consisted of Infantry Regiments. Their Division sign was the Black Cat and we had been linked up with them for the recent spring offensive. The Regiment made ready for the move during the evening of 10 May, so our party reloaded the store lorry, with just the bivouacs and bedding to be added. The tanks, on transporters, and crews moved away that night. They were to have two nights of travel.

The echelon of wheeled vehicles moved away northwards at 04:30 on 11 May and the order of convoy was HQ, A, B and C Squadrons. So our party on the store lorry was, as so often before, the tail-end vehicle.

Dawn was just breaking as we crossed the very long pontoon bridge over the Po River. We then moved on to the wide tarmac of Route 16 and passed through the town of Rovigo and then the much larger town of Padua. By now the sun was well up and travelling was a hot, tiresome and thirsty business. Our route swung eastwards and we struck the coast at Mestre. We had a good view of Venice lying a short distance out to sea from the mainland. It appeared in the haze of strong sunlight as if the buildings were floating on the bluest of blue waters.

A few miles beyond Venice one of our Squadron lorries had pulled up just off the road, so we did likewise. The lorry had developed a spot of engine trouble so, while Frank and 'Nix' worked on the engine, Charlie and I crashed on a brew and made a few spam sandwiches. When an hour later our two vehicles were ready to move off, a Red Cap Patrol told us to take Route 14 from the crossroads a mile or so up the road and continue for about another 70 miles. We proceeded on our way expecting to catch the convoy since they must have halted somewhere for lunch. However, we travelled on for many miles and never did come across them en-route.

We passed through Portogruaro and then, at Cervignano crossroads, we saw our Rhino-67 Regimental sign pointing left. Taking this road, we reached a small town called Palmanova and here saw members of an advance party billeted. We waited and it was more than an hour later when the Regiment's main convoy pulled in. It transpired that from the crossroads near Mestre the way was via Route 13, whereas we had come down Route 14, so they had come by way of Treviso and Udine.

Palmanova we found to be a quaint, fortified town having very high walls all around. These walls mostly took the form of high grassy banks and on the outside, running right around, was a deep moat. The four roads running into the town each crossed the moat by a narrow bridge and then through the walls by way of a narrow fortified archway. The town was an Italian garrison and it was in the barracks that most of the transport troops of our echelon were billeted. However, all the technical staff, including our party were billeted at the extensive garages situated quite apart from the barracks. The tanks and crews of the Regiment never turned up here and we understood them to be on some mission or other. George and Jock with the recovery tank and the 'Flying Fitters' in their armoured car were away with this tank force.

Alex turned up at Palmanova on 15 May and we were able to enjoy some time together. Alex had an interesting story to tell about his experiences since we last chatted together. He had left the echelon on 24 April to drive an officer down to Naples in the 15 cwt Bedford truck. On their return from Naples they stayed a night in Rome and then, quite unexpectedly, duty took them north to Genoa on the west coast. From there they had gone to Florence and back again to Rome. The last couple of nights had been spent at Bologna because the Bedford had developed some trouble and they pulled into some Army workshops there. Alex had been in Naples when the Italian surrender came and in Genoa on VE Day.

It was about mid May that the Government announced details of the British Forces release scheme. This, coupled with a previously notified scheme, granting 28 days' home leave for those in that part of the world who had not been abroad for more than three years, led to a lot of discussion. Many of the Regiment had now been abroad since setting sail from England three years and eight months previously. New intakes into the Regiment to bring it up to strength over these years had, most likely, not been abroad very long. A few of these, including Jack of our party, were already on their way home with the first group to have this period of 28 days' home leave. They would, of course, be returning afterwards.

At the same time as all this discussion, most of us were hoping and expecting that length of overseas service would be reduced from the present four and a half years to four years. If this should happen, then most of the Regiment would be due to return to England in a few months' time. In the meantime, we were all trying to work out just what number our own particular service release group would be. I made mine out to be Group 21. Judging by our letters from home, all these schemes must have been worrying and confusing to our wives, sweethearts and families back in Blighty.

Our first week at Palmanova was quiet because there was little needing to be done. Trips were started to the coast for sea bathing and so, during the week, I twice joined that party. The chosen spot was only about 14 miles away and was called Grado. It stood out from the main shore on an island, not so very large, and was reached by a road over a narrow causeway. In a way, I suppose, it was a smaller version of Venice. Grado boasted a small town area with many attractive small hotels, a beautiful little harbour and lots of boats. It also had a delightful sandy beach on the open side and the sea was calm, almost like a lagoon. In this lovely May weather, to say the bathing was smashing would be an understatement. It was superb!

One evening Len Goring and I went with a small party into Udine. There was nothing much there for troops but we found it to be quite a large town in a setting near the mountains. Back in Palmanova we all took to wearing KD again, casting aside the old battledress.

About this time, news to we ordinary squaddies began to trickle through regarding the mission of the tanks. They had been directed into the mountains to assist in patrolling the Morgan Line between Italy and Yugoslavia to help restrain the over-eager Marshall Tito from anticipating peace settlements. Stories came through that the Slav troops eventually offered to play our tank crews at football. This they did by day but still arrested the Slavs if they crossed the Line at night.

The second week of the Palmanova period included Whit Monday (21 May) so, after the mid-day lunch, more personnel than usual did the sea-bathing trip to Grado. Some of our party decided to go and, at the last moment, I went along too. Swimming on my back was my favourite method as I was always able to move about better in the water that way. I was doing just that and enjoying the warm calm water when I and another fellow collided. After finding bottom with our feet and having shaken the water from our eyes, we stared at each other in complete astonishment. Thus, on this Whit-Monday 1945, I met only the second person abroad I had known back home in England (or as we squaddies used to say, in Civvy Street). He was Les Warren and we had worked together in the Stock and Despatch Department of J S Fry & Sons for years. Les had been a first-aid man at the factory and for this reason had been called into the Army upon the outbreak of the war. We had last spoken together in the autumn of 1939 and he was last known by me to be at a large Military hospital at Netley near Southampton.

Well, we talked and talked as you can well imagine and it was of much interest to me to learn about several of our working friends – where they were serving, and so on. We spoke about Alf Fricker and his wife. We had both learned from home that Alf, being in the RAF and having passed out as a Pilot, had been shot down and killed somewhere in Europe. Les Warren had been abroad two years, having landed in North Africa near Algiers and moved to Italy. He was in a Field Ambulance Unit with the 56th Infantry Division, to whom our Regiment had been (and was at the time) attached from time to time in Italy.

Eventually we had to break off our talking since both Units' transport was aiming to be back for evening dinner. However, Les gave me his Unit's particulars so I promised to pay him a visit at some future date.

Rather late in the evening a mobile film unit turned up at Palmanova and so we enjoyed an open-air picture show.

Sagrado, near the Yugoslav border

A few days later the Regimental Echelon moved out of Palmanova. The move was only a short one of about six or seven miles and was towards the hills and mountains very close to the border with Yugoslavia.

We ended up at a small border town called Sagrado, which was more of a village really, situated on the narrowing coastal plain. Entering the town from the south, we drove over a long iron girder bridge that spanned a river. After doing so we soon turned right to enter a square, on two sides of which were barrack-like buildings. The echelon took over some of these barracks and of our party, Charlie, Frank and 'Nix' decided to take a room that had an entrance near to where our store lorry remained. This was handy, since fitters' tools and everything were stored in the lorry. There was a parking area for all the normal vehicles. I decided to remain on the lorry for sleeping as my homemade bed fitted in snugly. For quite a while now we had been sleeping under mosquito nets again, which was a bit of a nuisance but at least they kept the flies at bay.

In the early days in Sagrado there was some anxiety with regard to the Slavs. They liked to parade about the town and make a show. We were living side by side with them, with us mounting a guard at one end of the girder bridge at the town's entrance and them at the other end of the bridge. It was the same at other spots where guards were thought to be required.

When they held their daily parade it was something of a joke to us, since they looked a motley crowd dressed in all kinds of uniforms and some with no uniforms at all. There were a number of women soldiers as well. They carried a wide mixture of arms but at their belts they all had dangerous-looking daggers or knives. When walking out in the town we had to be clean and tidy but no arms were normally carried. I suppose this was to help to maintain confidence.

The river nearby was almost devoid of water although it was only the end of May. There was one place, however, where a large pool had formed so we used this, for a brief period, for bathing and sunbathing. In the ever-increasing hot sun this pool soon dried up, so we started using a canal that flowed along one side of the barrack grounds. Actually, there were several of these canals in the area. Once more we were all developing a nice brown tan.

On Friday evening 1 June, at the town's soccer ground, a Regimental XI including seven C Squadron 'boys' played a game versus the Lancashire Fusiliers of the 56th Division. It was a rousing game ending in a 3-all draw.

At the beginning of June the 56th (Black Cat) Division took over a number of the hotels at Grado, one of which was allotted to the 10th Royal Hussars. One Squadron of cooks moved in and so leave parties started of six per Squadron for a four-day period each.

About the 6th of the month all the Squadron's technical storemen were ordered up to the tanks' leaguering area. We were told to take working kit and bivouacs as we would be staying several days. The spot in the hills was delightful, near pinewoods and with wonderful views. Our job there was to check all equipment and tool kits of each tank. We held lists of what each tank had, or should have, these not necessarily being the same. No tank had the full list of tools anyway. Our Squadron's tanks now numbered about 12, being four below the usual establishment, and I had to check these. The work was done during the mornings only and was not rushed in any way, so we remained for several days.

The tanks were only up there as a precaution, so the crews were enjoying an easy time playing all sorts of games. I tried my hand with the cricket bat and also at beach tennis played by throwing a sizeable rubber ring. I don't know where all the games kit had come from. I was able to see George and Jock to have a chat as well as our 'Flying Fitters', all of whom were truly 'browned-off' except where they were covered by shorts!

One evening during the stay, a mobile film unit came and, after dusk, we had an open-air showing of 'Precious Cargo' featuring Robert Taylor and Charles Laughton.

The event that caused most excitement whilst I was there was the announcement over the air that 'overseas service' was being cut from four and a half years to four years. After VE Day we had all looked forward to two things; firstly the announcement of the Services Release Scheme and, secondly, the announcement of a reduction in the length of overseas service as had been promised when the European War was concluded.

The Release Scheme was by groups as stated before (I was in Group 21). Details were that, on Demob, a leave of 56 days on full pay and rations would be given. Furthermore, one day's leave with full allowances would be due for each month served abroad. Most of us reckoned we would be due to 104 days' leave, if not returning to England until the month of September. Someone jokingly remarked, "It would be a wonderful chance to have a nice long holiday abroad!"

There were a number of lectures explaining or confusing the details of schemes for home leave that were now in operation. There were service personnel who came under what was known as 'Python' who were those with less than six months to go before completing the full length of overseas service. Python people became ineligible for any home leave. In our Regiment some 30-40 percent came under this scheme.

There was the scheme called 'LILOP' (Leave In Lieu of Python) which was for 61 days' home leave. This suited the Regular Soldiers for it allowed them home leave followed by a return to their own Unit. Also, anyone could convert to LILOP by signing on for a further two years' service.

Then there was 'LIAP' (leave In Addition to Python). Alex and George came under this and would, after their Python leave of 28 days, have to serve for six months or so with some other Unit until their groups came up for release. I, being Group 21, was expected to only serve another month or six weeks in any case. Sergeant 'Blondy' Osborne, our Sergeant of the 'Flying Fitters' signed on for a further two years' service and was one of the first who went on the 61 days' leave. Others who took leave in the course of the next few months were Regulars like Sergeant Major 'Buck' Jones and Quartermaster 'Speedy' Archer from C Squadron.

One evening at the Regimental canteen, I got into conversation with Corporal Tomlinson. He had only just returned a few days earlier from 28 days' leave in England. His views about being home were as follows: – "You will find the younger element have grown up and the older people looking much older. You will see people who you knew well but will have to think hard to recall their names. You will find living indoors very stifling and will want to throw open your windows."

Towards the second week of June the Slav Troops had disappeared from the area, so they must have been withdrawn. What little tension there had been now eased, and on the 12th all tanks and other personnel returned from the hills to Sagrado. Everyone became settled in either the barrack-like buildings or in tents within the compound. Space was also available for the tanks to be lined up in rows. The 'Flying Fitters' moved into the room along with Charlie, Frank and 'Nix' and parked the armoured car right behind the store lorry. George and Jock were in a patrol tent not far away. There was a morning Parade by C Squadron around 08.00 but there were neither dress uniforms nor even the need to shave. It was more-or-less a kind of roll call. 'Buck' Jones gave our party a smiling tick-off more than once for not showing a leg and making an attempt to be on Parade. It was only a very brief affair anyhow.

Everyone was given plenty of freedom to play sports of all kinds, to bathe, or to just relax. However, I did have a few busy mornings. When the Regiment was corralled together it was always a busier time for me. For the purpose of becoming a Regiment of Occupation we had taken over some armoured cars and it was checking these for C Squadron which gave me some work. Sometime soon all the Squadron's tanks were to be handed over so that would be more work for me.

On 14 June the mobile film unit gave us another show which Alex and I went along to see. The picture was Bing Crosby in 'Going My Way' and it was very good. The Regiment had now taken in some reinforcements and in our Squadron I came across a pale face, a Trooper Johnson, who hailed from Lena Street, Easton, an area of Bristol.

CHAPTER TWENTY-SEVEN

KILLING TIME

June to August 1945

Relaxing

The 56th Division organised a short season of opera and this took place at an open-air theatre in the nearby small town of Gradisca. The show was by the Delfa Opera Company. On the evening of 17 June (my birthday) Alex and I went along and quite enjoyed Tosca though, of course, it was sung in Italian.

Another activity I never expected to take part in in Italy was cricket. There was a Squadron game on the afternoon of the 18th played on a coconut matting wicket, which C Squadron lost 79 runs to 68. However, I was pleased with my effort of 36 not out.

There were not many duties to be done, just a few morning lectures that were compulsory to attend. Everyone was having plenty of freedom to enjoy the grand sunshine, and lots of sport and entertainment was available. Maybe the new reinforcements were doing the necessary duties. There was one small cinema in Sagrado and there, about twice a week, English talkies were shown.

We began to learn that Sevicemen going home on the 28-day leave scheme from Italy were doing so by an overland route across Europe. The route from Italy was via Klagenfurt in the Carinthian part of Austria, where the big Alamein Transit Camp was set up. Rumours floating around through the weeks had the Python people going home by three possible routes. One was as just described, another was by overland train from Milan and yet another was by ship from Naples. During the last week of June another small party departed via the overland route for the UK. These were non-Python troops, some of whom had only been abroad for two years. After 28 days' leave they would be returning to Italy to rejoin the Regiment. Of course, many of us were nearing four years abroad and itching to get home; however, when it did come we would only have a one-way ticket.

The Squadron played two cricket matches the following week. Monday was against the unbeaten A Squadron and, batting first we made 84, which was considered good. I scored 25. Then we bowled them all out for 52 so had a good win. Tuesday's game was against HQ Squadron, thought to be easy-meat, but after getting them out for 62, our side collapsed to 31 all out, of which I notched 11 and was last man out. That same day in the evening I turned out for the weakened Squadron soccer team and we lost 4-1. It was so hot I swore to myself not to play in Italy again.

Right at the end of the month I was instructed to report to Technical Office in HQ Squadron, which resulted in me having to do a spot of work. This was the half-yearly census of stores and fitters' special tools held in my store lorry. It kept me busy for at least a day.

Most evenings of the first week of July, George and I went for walks, the favourite stroll being up the river to the little township of Gradisca, no more than two miles away. Gradisca was a smart and clean-looking place and the houses seemed new. In the centre was a large common that was lined with horse chestnut trees, giving it an English appearance. On the main street facing the common was a row of neat shops and as one of these was an ice-cream bar we decided to treat ourselves. In the square, formed by crossroads, the common and buildings, we noticed a new Army sign had been erected and it read "Eighth Army Blighty Leave Route" and had an arrow pointing up the Udine road.

Nearby was the football ground, a nice level pitch, and being below the level of three roads skirting it, quite a banking was formed between the road level and the pitch. It was a ground open to these roads and not enclosed in any way. The Italians played skilful football from what we had seen. They took the game very seriously and became most excitable. The evenings when a match was on were like local gala nights, for everybody turned up, males and females too and, of course, many of the troops stationed in the area.

On the first Sunday evening of July an Italian Civil XI played the 56th Division. Two 10th Royal Hussars men, both from C Squadron played in the Division's team. They were Moore, ex-Chesterfield goalkeeper, and a chap named Parfitt from the Shepton Mallet area who had played for the town's team. He played at inside right. There must have been a couple of thousand of us watching the game. The Italian XI wore blue sleeveless shirts, very brief white shorts and little ankle socks just showing above their boots. The Italian outside left, we understood, was an international player by the name of Bruno. The shirts they wore also had numbers on the back – this was new to us. 56th Division XI played in all white with a black cat motif on the breast of the shirts. It was a very good game with seven goals scored, and didn't the Italians (both players and spectators) get excited when they twice took the lead! However, it was 56th Division who ran out winners 4-3 and Parfitt notched the one that counted near the end. After the game George and I had an ice, then strolled back by way of the dead straight road to Sagrado.

During that week, early in July, I played for the Squadron in two further cricket games. One of these was won and the other lost and my knocks were 32 and 8 respectively.

It was great to be enjoying the Italian summer in the way we were and many of us, for the fourth summer following, were well and truly 'browned off' with regard to the colour of our skin.

On Tuesday 10 July the Regiment held a Sports Contest in Trieste and plenty of our transport was made available for those wishing to go. Many did go but George and I spent a quiet time swimming and sunbathing in the afternoon. The bathing in the canal (the river by now had dried up) was right on our doorstep, so we used to go in our trunks all ready for the plunge. That evening ended up being very noisy in our quarter of the barracks, since C Squadron were celebrating having won the Regimental Shield at the sports. The canteen was doing a roaring trade with its sales of wine and the Shield was on display there. It bore the Regiment's badge and the wording, "Regimental Sports Trieste Italy 1945".

Our Squadron had another cricket match on the Thursday and it was so hot, as it had been all week, that most of us played wearing only bathing trunks. As soon as the game ended we were in the canal. The heat at this time made sleeping difficult. I was still using the lorry at night so I lay on the bed under the mosquito net wearing only pants and no covering. One blanket cover had been enough for a long time anyway.

On the Saturday evening 19 July, George and I had a steady stroll up to Gradisca and, while George went for the ices, I went in for a haircut nearby. That Italian barber certainly made a meal of me. He fussed and I fumed, and he shoved a white cloth further round and down my neck – at least it caught some of the sweat that dripped off me. Was I thankful to eventually rejoin George and what remained of the ice cream!

About the third week in the month, evening dances began in a small hall in the town. These continued about two or three times a week and were attended by some of the locals as well as by servicemen. During this period I attended two of these and once tried a dance with Jimmy of the 'Flying Fitters'.

On the Thursday of that week the Regiment took on the 9th Lancers at cricket. Several of our Squadron players were included in the side, one of whom was Alan Hartley. He captained our Squadron XI and also the Regimental XI and, in the game, proved our hero by making 41 not out in a game we won by one wicket. I failed to trouble the scorers this time! Alan Hartley was a schoolteacher in Civvy Street and came from Blackpool.

Another evening that week George and I hitchhiked to Gorizia for a change. This was a sizeable town some 12 miles distant, to the north and close to the Yugoslav border. From a distance it appeared that the town lay directly at the foot of the huge range of mountains. We only stayed for a short time since the shops were closed and there wasn't much sign of life.

On the third Sunday of July in Gradisca there was a big evening Fiesta, part of the proceedings being a repeat soccer match between the 56th Division and an Italian Civil XI. George, 'Nix', Jimmy and I went along with a big crowd of servicemen and Italian locals of both sexes. To help create the carnival atmosphere, a Military Pipe Band of, I believe the Guards Brigade, was in attendance. The game was a good one which 56th Division won 5-2.

The next morning at 09:15 I turned out at soccer for the Squadron in a League game that was jolly hot, even at that time of day. Our Squadron won 5-0 and I was fortunate to perform the unusual feat of scoring the first goal direct from a corner kick. Because of the very hot weather conditions, these Squadron League games lasted only an hour. In the game just mentioned I cast off my boots for the last 15 minutes or so because they were such a poor fit and were hurting my feet on the bone-hard ground. Incidentally, all football boots were drawn from a store and handed back after the game but cricket was played in the Army plimsolls that all personnel possessed.

At Udine the following day I was employed in the 'handing over' of an armoured car to an ADS Centre. The Commander, driver and I were collected by Alex in the same old Bedford 15cwt truck and taken back to our Unit.

Several of us rarely went to bed before midnight. We would all return from our various ways of spending the evening and then sit about talking. Much of the talk at this time would be about the old, old question of getting back home to England. When would we go and how would we travel? There were so many different rumours and tales doing the rounds that this was still anyone's guess. Anyhow, we found going to bed early didn't mean sleep. The hot weather prevented this unless we were extremely tired.

Towards the end of July I played in a cricket game that was to decide the Squadron Championship. It was HQ Squadron versus C. We batted first and quickly lost three wickets for two runs but thanks in the main to Alan Hartley who made 20, we managed to go on to 59. HQ had reached 22 when their first wicket fell and they then collapsed to 39 for 8 wickets. Afterwards they recovered a little but in a breathless over, their last two wickets fell without them being able to get the one run needed for victory and so it was a tie.

Another contest had been played out the day before in England. We heard the result, which was a decisive win for Labour over Conservatives.

Grado and Sagrado

The last Sunday in July brought the start of a four-day leave on the coast at Grado. George and I and a few others, travelled down in the morning. The trip was of about 20 miles. We were accommodated in a spacious hotel where some of the Regiment's cooks, assisted by a few Italians, provided the meals. George and I shared a bedroom on the third floor with two single beds. It was a neat little room with washbasin, wardrobe and small table. There were glass doors leading to a small balcony that had a sea view. The weather was such that these doors remained open throughout our stay. The dining room was on the ground floor and the meals proved to be very good indeed.

A long afternoon was spent on the beach where a group of us paid ten Lire for a colourful tent. In the main, the tents were used to provide some shade from the burning sun. Many people, not only servicemen but also Italian civilians, were enjoying the beach and bathing. The Italian females looked attractive in their scant bikinis. The sea here was very calm and we could go out for a long way and still touch bottom. But perhaps what impressed us most was the warmth of the water – just grand! The beach was of silver sand and, lying on it, we got covered because in the sun our bodies never dried, either they were wet with seawater or damp with perspiration. All in all it was a most picturesque scene with many yachts with sails of every conceivable colour.

That Sunday evening George and I went to a service at a little mission. We, plus two others, formed the congregation and afterwards had a talk with the other two. They were an elderly English couple in Italy working for Toc H. The wife remarked that the beach here would be paradise for children back home. They told us that they had two sons and so expressed concern that we should get home soon.

On the beach, the next afternoon, was quite a large number of 10th Royal Hussars (including Alex) who had arrived that morning. A few of us went to an open-air cinema in the evening with the show starting after dusk at 21:30 hours.

On Sunday morning 5 August, Jock Spiers was due to depart for 28 days' leave in Blighty. George and I had fully enjoyed the break at Grado but returned to the Barracks at Sagrado just in time to wish Jock (and the Recovery Tank with George) a good send-off. Most of our party did not expect to see Jock again because it was assumed we would have left for home before he returned to the Regiment. Jock had to serve about another eight months before his release. Jock insisted on making a list of all our party's addresses before leaving. We all knew he was from Airdrie in Scotland and George and I also knew that he was an ex-boy and officer of the 1st Company of Chapelhall Boys' Brigade.

About this time in a letter to my wife, I expressed the view that the short break at Grado had done me good since I did not now feel quite so 'cheesed off' at us still 'kicking our heels' out in Italy.

Monday 6 August was a Bank Holiday but for us there was only one notable event and this affected only a selected few of the Regiment, including George. It was a parade by the troops in the area with an inspection by General Alexander. This was held at Palmanova in the afternoon.

The same morning I reported sick because of concern about a rash around my middle. At the MO's I found Len Goring and others reporting the same problem.

Next day on Orders bathing in the canal was banned and all water now had to be boiled prior to use. Len Goring, a few others and I had to report for treatment to a Field Ambulance Unit in the Palmanova area. At the Ambulance Unit I met up again with Les Warren, for it happened to be his section and they were also attached to 56th Division. We all received treatment and were told it should not be necessary to go again.

The rest of the 10th 'boys' went off back in the truck but I was invited by Les to stay for dinner and a chat. Maybe Les had some influence on the Unit's cooks because the dinner was first class – tinned turkey and chips with other trimmings, to say nothing of the dessert. At some point during our chat the subject of 'ears and hearing' cropped up. This resulted in Les giving my ears a thoroughly good syringe since I felt they could do with it. All the dust and sand of the 8th Army travels came out, it would seem!

The next few days of August saw a major change in the weather and we experienced thundery showers. George and I went to a couple of evening shows instead of for walks. One of the pictures we saw was 'This Happy Breed'. However, the sunshine soon returned and one morning I was called on to play soccer again for the Squadron Team because a couple of the team regulars were on leave.

Recently in our newspaper, 'Eighth Army News', there had been a campaign against the daily press in England printing inaccurate information about Home Leave and Army Release. This had been over a period of time and the campaign had been started because of an avalanche of letters from troops which had been triggered off because of letters from home conveying confusion and anxiety. The Far East War came to an end about this time and it was soon announced that demobilisation would be speeded up.

Mid-month saw the 56th Division again arrange a short season of opera at the open-air theatre at Gradisca. This was staged by La Scala Opera Company of Milan and included both the orchestra and chorus of this theatre. On Saturday evening 11th August, George and I fully enjoyed the opera 'La Traviata'. The open-air theatre was a most delightful setting and although the performances were timed to start at dusk, the area was floodlit. Once the orchestra started up the arena floodlights went out and normal stage lighting took over.

On Monday 13 August, 'Nix' and I went into Trieste for the day. The road from Sagrado joined up to Route 14 at Monfalcone and from there ran along the coast between the face of mountains and, in places, a sheer drop into the sea. Here and there the road ran through tunnels but otherwise sunlit seascapes were always in view and the Adriatic was a deep rich blue. It was my first visit to this city and seaport and I was surprised that it was so large a place. The shops and markets were full of goods and certainly there seemed to be no shortages. However, most of these things were quite expensive. City life appeared to be very normal and there was some shipping standing off in the bay, with smaller boats in the harbour.

Quite early on Wednesday the 15th we heard over the air that the day had been declared 'VJ Day' but it was 10: 00 before the order came through that the Regiment would take a holiday until the Friday. Our Squadron canteen opened soon after. It had been decorated with flags and some of the boys were merry even before lunchtime. After this lunch, George and I linked up with HQ Technical Staff who were going by truck into Grado for bathing. We had a smashing time together, both in and out of the sea, arriving back for a late dinner at 19:00 hours.

George and I had pre-booked for the opera that evening so after a quick dinner and a brush-up we walked up to Gradisca. We had booked slightly better seats for that evening, 250 Lire (60p). The large theatre was packed out, for the Italians were making it a Fiesta too and the excitable chatter and laughter only died out to complete silence when Alfredo Simonetto, the Conductor, took his place before the 80-piece orchestra. The opera was Rigoletto and it was the best I had seen so far. The voice of the young soprano, who played the part of Gilda, was beautiful. We heard she was in her first year of lead parts and the name was kept off the programmes. Anyway, she 'brought the house down' in the solo 'Tutti le feste al tempio' (On every festal morning) and again in the duet with Rigoletto (Aye, my soul, nought but vengeance desiring).

For the night of the 16/17 August I was NCO of the Regimental Guard, so most of the 16th was spent in doing a bit of the Army spit and polish. This was something quite rare for me. Indeed I don't suppose I took part in any more than seven or eight guards in the whole of my four years abroad. It was the same for the whole of our party and the 'Flying Fitters' because it seemed generally accepted that tradesmen of the Regiment would be exempt, as we were for most parades. It may have been a policy right throughout the Army, I don't really know. However, the Guard Mounting (a night guard only) at Sagrado involved marching the guard through the little town's main street so we had to be reasonably smart. This guard too was mounted with our troops wearing a holster and carrying a ·38 revolver. Revolvers were the personal arms of most of the Regiment but some of the echelon drivers, from time to time, carried rifles. I know the echelons on the Western Desert used to mount a guard with rifles but it was much more the custom for the Regiment's guards to carry revolvers. Our night guard went off without incident.

On Tuesday 21 August my letter home to my wife contained the following: "Excitement is running high amongst us Python chaps of the Regiment because we do know, though nothing has appeared on Orders, that our Movement Order and Papers have come through. There are other significant happenings too. For two days I have been 'handing over' to the new C Squadron Technical Storeman. We've had to check the wheeled vehicles' tools and all stores and fitters' special tools held in our store lorry. The Squadron is now without any tanks, only a few armoured cars, so that is a good thing. I have now cleared right out of the lorry, moving my bed and personal belongings in with Charlie, 'Nix' and the rest."

That afternoon there was a grand and thrilling soccer match, 10th Royal Hussars versus Royal Artillery in the semi-final of the 56th Division Cup, which we won 3-2. We were all very hoarse from yelling in support and hoped the final would be played before we all left.

In the evening there was a function in the Squadron canteen – a farewell party for the Squadron Pythonites. We all thought we knew the date of our move and hoped to be in England by the 10 September or before. I finished my letter started in the morning: "Please do not write any further letters to me in CMF." The very writing of CMF made me realise we had had three main addresses in the four years we had been abroad. They were – 21 months as MEF (Middle East Forces), 10 months as BNAF (British North African Forces) and the last 17 months as CMF (Central Mediterranean Forces).

The day after this letter home on the 21st we had a medical, handed in KD uniforms, returned to battledress and then packed up our own kit. Lastly, we had a personal interview with the Commanding Officer (Lt Colonel D R B Kaye) who I found most pleasant in an informal chat. When I entered his caravan office he remarked, "Ah, this is another familiar face we shall miss seeing around" and went on to say, "Bristol has had much bombing, are all your folks all right…?" etc, etc. He asked me if I knew the Reverend Blackburn of Bristol Cathedral and several other questions regarding Bristol. Then there was the 'Goodbye' handshake.

After lunch on the 24 August (a Friday), Jimmy, 'Nix' and I suddenly decided to go into Trieste, so we went to the vehicle park and 'borrowed' a truck. George would not come, saying, "I'm not risking that mountain road at this stage". We only stayed in the city about an hour, long enough to buy one or two small gifts to take home.

The next evening (Saturday) and still being with the Regiment, George and I hitchhiked up river to Gorizia. We were more impressed with the town this time and it struck us as a centre for mountain lovers. We saw one group of men wearing alpine hats and expected at any moment to hear a yodelling chorus.

As the weekend was upon us again, we became cocksure our journey home would begin on Monday morning. One of these times our guess would be sure to come right! We were really groping in the dark. There were still numerous rumours as to the manner and route of travelling, just as over the past days, weeks and even months.

PART IV

BACK TO BLIGHTY

CHAPTER TWENTY-EIGHT

THE LONG JOURNEY TO ENGLAND

August 1945

On Monday, 27 August, sometime in the morning, the large group of the Regiment's Python men gathered together. They were our last moments of being associated with the 10th Royal Hussars, although many of us still wore the badge for many weeks to come. We were all excited and happy to be starting out at last on the journey back to England after four long years abroad.

Even at this late hour it was anyone's guess as to how we might travel. For the first few miles of our trip we were taken in the Regiment's lorries northwards, but this ended at a railway siding in Udine. Here there was a great buzz of anticipation and activity as all the Python men of the Brigade gathered. The train standing in the near siding was of the old familiar box trucks and it was into these that we eventually had to entrain. As the train moved out, many of the lorry drivers and a number of officers gave us a cheer. My brain failed to register who my companions were in the box truck, but it's certain that the 14 or so of us present were all 10th Royal Hussars.

The train did not hurry but maintained a regular slow speed in a generally southerly direction, stopping at regular intervals. On one such stop, lunch was served to us and it was then that a chap from the 9th Lancers made some enquiries for me as a result of which I had a brief meeting with the brother of Mrs H Skeyes (Rev Skeyes was the Minister of my home church). We had never met previously but letters used to mention Mrs Skeyes' brother having almost identical wartime experiences. Then later, on hearing he was in the 9th Lancers it explained things, since they were one of the three Armoured Regiments of the Brigade.

Our train plodded on and now a new rumour was doing the rounds. It was possible that we might go home by air. Well, the overland route home was becoming less of a possibility because every mile was taking us away from the northern part of Italy. At about 19:00 we were all being served dinner and mugs of tea at Rimini Station where we had been ordered to change trains.

Some two hours later we were aboard a posh passenger train as it pulled out from Rimini and so we travelled further and further south overnight. Some may have slept a little but I don't think I did, except perhaps for the last 100 miles.

We travelled many miles down the Adriatic coast where,

for the most part, the railway ran almost on the seashore. Standing and staring out of the window I especially looked out for the town of Ortona and was able to recognise it when it came into view. My mind wandered back a year to when, in the early days of August 1944, a small group of us from the Regiment had spent some time there. I also remembered the quiet beach where Alex and I enjoyed many hours bathing. In fact, to gain access to the beach, one crossed this very railway line at a small pedestrian level crossing. Being content at having seen Ortona I think sleep overtook me, for it was then after 02:00 in the wee small hours.

Our 250 mile train journey from Rimini, plus the 170 miles from Udine to Rimini, ended at a small town called Foggia in southeast Italy. Daylight had broken some time before we reached Foggia. Soon, trucks conveyed us a short way out of town to where a big RAF Station was situated. After a cooked breakfast, we were taken to billets (large wooden huts) that contained bunk beds, so it seemed possible that we might be there for a while, though it was now clear that we would reach England by air.

The next day we all filed through an office to sign certain papers. It could have been that these were something to do with air travel but I really don't remember. We also had to hand in more of our kit, followed by a lecture on the 'do's and don'ts' of air travel by bomber 'plane.

We were then split up into groups of about 60 with the aim that each group would be flown home within a period of four or five days. Thus, one group departed on Wednesday 29th and another on Thursday 30th. Each of these groups was given a flight number and also divided into smaller groups of 15 people and labelled A, B, C and D. I was in the flight number to depart on Friday the 31st and was in group D under a Sergeant Withers formerly of the Transport Troop of C Squadron.

After lunch we were all ready to depart, watching as the four Halifax Bombers came in to land. Some time passed before an announcement came over the loudspeaker system. It stated our flight number and continued: "Will groups A, B and C come on to the runway. Group D of the flight may have to be cancelled as one of the aircraft has developed a problem".

So group D party broke up and I went straight into a small canteen nearby where Alex was sitting at a table on his own. He remarked, "Don't look so glum, you'll get home in the end". Alex went to a counter and fetched two cups of tea and we sipped at these while chatting. Before our teas had been drunk, however, an announcement came over the speaker system calling for D party to hurry to the runway as the aircraft was now serviceable. I do not recall even pausing to wish Alex a "Cheerio" but dashed to pick up my kit and join the others hurrying along the tarmac. Alex's flight was due to depart the next day, Saturday, I believe.

Our group had to sit out evenly on the floor of the aircraft for take-off but afterwards we were not so restricted. Soon the Commander of the Crew came back to speak to us and invited us to have 15 minute periods, two men at a time, up forward with the Crew. There were no windows in the body of the aircraft but we were soon told, "We are now passing over Rome". Eventually Sergeant Withers and I went forward and it was like being in a large glass dome. We were then flying over the Mediterranean Sea, the sky was clear and we were in sunshine. Looking down, it was interesting to see the 'plane's shadow on the water. Before we had returned to the body of the aircraft we saw land up ahead. This was somewhere in the south of France and very soon we crossed the low sandy-looking shoreline. Then we could see the 'plane's shadow hurrying across fields, hedges and woods and it gave us some idea of our speed.

Sergeant Withers and I enjoyed a second brief spell up front. It was again sea below us, the Pilot said, "English Channel", but it was now very cloudy indeed and the water looked black. The plane hurried out of a cloud and we rushed over a coastline of dark rocky cliffs. We then had to withdraw to resume sitting on the 'plane's floor.

Very soon we landed and quickly had two feet on English soil.

CHAPTER TWENTY-NINE

BACK ON HOME SOIL

August to November 1945

Cornwall to Catterick

It was early evening on Friday, 31 August 1945 when we landed back in England. We were rushed into RAF buildings and in no time at all were linked up with the rest of our flight and enjoying a jolly good dinner at the RAF Mess. The crew of the flight joined us at this meal but they soon dashed away carrying raincoats and suitcases, probably because they were on a weekend leave.

After dinner, we were given an update on our immediate future and we discovered we had landed at RAF St Mawgan in Cornwall. We would next have to report to the Royal Armoured Corps depot at Catterick in Yorkshire. We would be travelling by train, being taken by trucks to the station in about one and a half hours' time. "In the meantime", said the officer, "You are given the freedom of the RAF canteen".

Our party of 60 or thereabouts flocked to the canteen and excitedly spent the time. Many had drinks at the bar while others were content with tea and a 'wad'. Many of us bought a plain postcard and a stamp in order to drop a line home. Buying stamps was something we'd have to get used to because mail home from abroad had been free for such a long time.

All too soon, three RAF lorries pulled up near the canteen and we were escorted on to these and taken to the railway station. No name boards were, as yet, displayed but I recognised it to be Newquay. There was no train at the platform so I wrote my postcard home while waiting, as follows:-

"Friday August 31

Dearest Love

Arrived by air this evening, landing in Cornwall. Am travelling all night to a Depot in Yorkshire, via London, and hope to be home in a day or so.

This is being written at Newquay and I expect to post it en-route. Everything OK and hope same with you.

Nice English drizzly rain to greet us.

*Love
Vince xx"*

Daylight was giving way to darkness as our train pulled away from Newquay with our group occupying a central coach. In our compartment there was talk for some while but, gradually this lessened as one and another dropped off to sleep. I was one who slept, but for how long I do not know.

It may have been the banging of carriage doors that woke me but the train had stopped and I became conscious of people moving about outside the train. We were at a station and a number of soldiers and sailors were getting off the train. Suddenly I had a thought. I jumped down to the platform, stopped a soldier and asked, "Would you mind posting this postcard for me?" He remarked, "Well, I've got to catch another train but maybe there's a post-box about here" and with that he was gone.

Then I really woke up – to the fact that our train had halted in Temple Meads, the central station in my home city of Bristol. Of course I had to tell someone and so those in our compartment were soon all awake. It turned out to be quite a halt too, about 30 minutes between 02:00 and 02:30 on 1 September. Eventually our train was on the move again and our compartment quickly returned to slumberland.

Paddington Station was quiet when we arrived there about 06:00 and for a while we stood about chatting. Soon, however, we filed past mobile catering units, receiving hot soup and sandwiches. There was another spell of just standing around before a couple of big Army lorries backed on to the station and we had to quickly climb aboard. We rode, without being able to see much, over to Kings Cross Station forecourt. It was about 08:00 then and the main departure platform was very much alive. As far as possible we stayed together in a large group while an officer went to the busy booking offices. A very long train was standing at the platform packed with mostly civilians but with some uniformed personnel. Up front a huge engine was slowly backing on to the coaches when our officer came dashing back to the group. He shouted, "Get on this train anywhere you can, as quickly as you can, and be sure to alight at Darlington". I well recall that three or four of our group never made the train, having gone to a stall to buy cigarettes; however, they did reach Catterick several hours after the main party.

On the train we were crammed shoulder to shoulder in the corridor and three of my travelling companions, big powerful Scots, wore the Merchant Navy uniform. No doubt they had recently enjoyed a few drinks because they were excitable and talkative. We were in a corridor on the east side of the train and remained standing thus the entire 250-mile journey to Darlington. In a way these three Scots made the trip interesting because from them I discovered they were travelling home to Aberdeen on leave and that this train was a good one to catch, with only four stops between Kings Cross and Edinburgh. I was told that the first stop would be Grantham in Lincolnshire where a lot of RAF people would hope to board the train. They did too, but I don't know how they squeezed in. The talking continued as one landmark after another was pointed out to me, this part of England being new to me.

When our train left York after a stop, my companions informed me that 50 minutes would see us in Darlington. Darlington Station was a busy place but our group soon linked up together and crossed to another platform where a little three-coach train stood almost empty and we were glad to be seated. This was the local train to Richmond, some 12 miles distant, from where Army trucks conveyed us the mile or two up the hill to Catterick Camp main office.

The time was now in the region of 14:15 hours and our first priority was to have a meal of some sort. This was provided in due course at the main dining area. Here our party officer told us that owing to arriving on a Saturday afternoon and the Camp staff being short-handed because of weekend leave and sport, it would be doubtful if they could cope with getting the party away on their 28 days' leave that day. However, he said they intended to try by all means to do so.

Following this, there were long periods of tiresome waiting interspersed with spells of activity, which involved such things as:

1. Filing through a Quartermaster's Store to have old uniforms, boots or hats replaced with new (I had a new hat).

2. Filing through another store for our 28 days' rations of fags, chocolate, sweets, soap, razor blades, etc.

3. Having a tea break.

4. Filing past the main office to be handed a 28 days' Leave Pass and Food Ration Coupons. Later, again filing past this same office to receive Rail Travel Warrants.

Home on 28 Days' Leave

Our group of 60 had spent slightly over six hours at Catterick Camp before returning to Richmond Station by Army trucks. We all caught the local train back to Darlington Station and there were then many excitable "Cheerios" and "Best of Lucks" as we split up into small groups of two or three, or even dispersing individually to all parts of the UK.

It was about 21:30 by then and I thought of perhaps catching a train via Sheffield and Birmingham. There were two others of the party making the same enquiries. One was for Bristol as I was, and the other for

Swansea. It was no good, as we had missed the last train by that route for the day so had to travel via London. There were other groups of our party also going back to London, perhaps to reach any of the southern counties, but we three kept together. The next train for London was, I think, 23:10 so there was plenty of time to look around.

In the six or eight weeks after my 28 days' leave, I used Darlington Station quite a bit and felt sure that thousands of servicemen, like me, felt very thankful for the Women's Voluntary Service. A large refreshment stall at one end of the main platform was open and run 24 hours a day by these ladies. Also a number of refreshment trolleys manned by them met the trains that called at the Station at any time of day or night.

We used their refreshment stall and enjoyed tea and sandwiches some time between 22:00 and 22:30. The three of us watched several trains depart for various destinations and noted how the non-stop expresses went up and down on a set of lines just by-passing the station. We were, however, very glad when the overhead electric sign lit up with the message 'Next train this platform – Kings Cross'.

So, for the second night in a row I spent my time travelling by rail as we journeyed back to Kings Cross. We three found a compartment with space and soon found we had barged in on four females travelling from Newcastle to London. Two of these were WRENs in uniform and the other two were rather elderly. We must have told them our story and that we were on our second night of travel because, before York was reached, we had corner seats and the elderly ladies' travelling rugs! Small wonder I remember little of that journey until approaching Kings Cross Station.

The concern of the three of us then was to get over to Paddington as soon as possible, so we went straight to Kings Cross Underground Station only to find gates barring the entrance. Someone told us, "It's Sunday morning, and the underground trains don't start 'til 8 o'clock". We realised that it was not yet even 06:00 so, looking about the area, we discovered an all-night cafe and some of our 'boys' already having breakfast. We also were soon having a hearty meal and lashings of tea, taking our time in the warm, cosy little place.

How we three travelled over to Paddington in the end I cannot recall but I know we reached there well before 08:00. We all went into the toilets and had a jolly good wash. Just adjoining was a barber's shop, so we went in for a shave and were probably his first customers that morning. I seem to remember buying a newspaper.

Our train backed into a platform quite early so we boarded it and made ourselves comfortable. Very few people used that train so we had the compartment to ourselves for the whole trip to Temple Meads, where the three of us bid each other, "Cheerio".

Coming out of the station I noticed a few taxis and decided that was the way to get home. So it was, I arrived back at home at about lunchtime on Sunday, 2 September.

It was an emotional reunion with my wife and six year old son, Colin, and a happy surprise for them to have me arrive so early in the month. My wife told me that

Colin was in the front room when the taxi arrived. He went trotting into the kitchen where my wife was preparing lunch saying, "Mummy, there's a soldier at the gate".

In the seven days since leaving the Regiment at Sagrado in Italy I had travelled around 1,560 miles by train and, I suppose, a similar number of miles by air.

There was a good welcome home by relatives and friends and several parties were held. I often think about and am thankful for all the hundreds of letters received from my wife, relatives and friends while I was overseas. Some of these came to me from countries other than England, including India, South Africa, Palestine, Italy and other parts of Europe. In the same four-year period I estimate having written in the region of 600 letters, the ones to my wife having been numbered from 1 to 249. I also wrote 17 long letters of my experiences.

An invitation to a wedding was received after a few days and so, on 14 September (a Friday), my wife, Colin and I travelled to Brixham in South Devon. We stayed overnight and attended the marriage at All Saints Church of my great army pal Alex Watts to Susan Stamp. After the wedding we went to Paignton to stay for one week's holiday from 15 to 22 September, which had been booked after receiving the invitation from Alex and Susan.

My leave came to an end on Monday 1 October when I caught the 19:30 Newcastle train back to Darlington and the early morning local train to Richmond. My leave actually ended by being due back at Catterick Camp by 08:00 hours on 2 October.

Back to Catterick Camp and then Home to Bristol

Within a few days all those who left the Regiment together turned up at Catterick. What Alex had told us at Brixham was confirmed, namely that each air group home had landed at different RAF Stations in England. All those in the bigger party, who's Demob Group was under 23, moved to a different part of the Camp some half a mile away. This included me and we were housed in a row of large Nissen Huts, each hut containing a group. So all of those in my hut were Group 21 for release. My old friends, Alex Watts and George Bull, had a while longer to serve so remained in the normal part of Camp and I did not see so much of them from that point, unless bumping into them casually on an evening at a canteen. They were both eventually posted away from Catterick back into Europe.

Of those in Group 21 hut, I linked up with Corporal Ainsworth. Harry had always been one of C Squadron's Quartermasters' party, so we knew each other quite well. We shared a bunk bed with him on the bottom one. He was also made Corporal in charge of the hut. There was a good reason why Harry had always been with the Quartermaster staff of our Squadron. It was because in Civvy Street he had been a sign writer and the Regiment used him for painting all signs required on vehicles, etc. Our signs had required red, white and black paint and I had often obtained supplies for him. 'Nix' Graham, another old pal, was in release Group 20 and so was in the next hut.

There were only minor duties to be done over this period, mostly to do with helping the cookhouse staff by way of 'spud bashing' and washing the many dishes after meals. Other than this we were free to come and go as we pleased within a small area.

The cookhouse duties tied me, so Harry gave me the duty of keeping the hut clean. Thereafter, he and I often went off into Richmond at about 10:30. In the cobbled market square we had a favourite cafe where a lot of time was spent and we found it an interesting little town to look around. Sometimes we would walk a short way up the dale. Swaledale always looked attractive from the castle ruins. Other times we would spend hours together at one or other of the many Camp clubs.

One week, for a change, many of us went on loan to farms in quite a wide area. We would be taken out to these farms early morning and collected about teatime. I went out on this duty for just five days and our particular farm used us for collecting sugar beet and swedes. We were provided with a traditional farm lunch of bread and cheese.

On several Saturdays, Harry, 'Nix' and I went into Darlington for most of the day and on two occasions saw football matches at the Town's little ground. League games had not then resumed so they were only 'friendly' ones that we saw. One was versus Bradford City and the other Barnsley.

Some of those who lived not too distant managed to obtain a few weekend passes. One of these was Harry, who lived in Blackburn. I had just one weekend pass during the period and this was on Saturday 27 October. Leaving Catterick at 14:00, I did not reach home until 01:15 on Sunday. Changing at York, I caught a train via Derby and Birmingham but found it ran no further than Gloucester which meant a long wait before a train came for Bristol.

From this leave I returned on Monday evening, 29 October, catching the 19:30 Newcastle train again. This train was so packed that I, along with the others, had to sit on the floor of the corridor for most of the night journey. My Pass expired at 08:00 hours on the Tuesday.

There was a Saturday when 'Nix' and I had a day in Newcastle. The main reason for us going was a friendly soccer game, which was Newcastle versus Liverpool. This had been written up in our newspapers all week. I also told 'Nix' about Phil Taylor who was due to play for Liverpool.

We reached Darlington Station soon after 10:30 and almost at once bumped into 'Buck' Jones (C Squadron Sergeant Major). He was waiting for a London-bound train on his way to rejoin the Regiment after a home leave. He was quite chatty and interested to hear where we were going. 'Buck' told us he would rejoin the Regiment now based in Austria.

'Nix' and I reached Newcastle and had a look around before going in somewhere for lunch. We went quite early to St James' Park and stood in the enclosure next to the tunnel from which the players emerged, so had a really close-up view of Phil Taylor. Philip Taylor was a Bristolian brought up in Carlyle Road and he went through the Boys' Brigade of my church. He had also played a few games in the church soccer team I played for but his main amateur team was Bristol St George before signing as a professional for Bristol Rovers who, in turn, sold him to Liverpool. In later years he captained Liverpool and one season led them out at Wembley in a Cup Final. On this day at Newcastle, however, Liverpool received a trouncing. 'Nix' and I spent a few hours at a club before returning to Darlington and thence Catterick.

There came a day, 15 November in fact, when early one morning those of us in Release Group 21 (our hut) were paraded and taken by lorries to Darlington Station. We all travelled by train to York where, at some special depot near the Station we were split up into groups according to our home area. Thus it was "Cheerio" between Corporal Ainsworth and me.

A fair-sized party of South West Englanders left very much later that day for Taunton. It became night travel once again and so it was nearly breakfast time when Taunton was reached. After a meal we passed through the Demob Centre, casting off battledress and Army boots, etc, replacing them with our personally chosen civilian suit, shoes and hat. We were given a Rail Warrant to our home town and, if memory serves me correctly, Food Ration Cards lasting a period of time.

SO I REACHED HOME, ONCE MORE A CIVILIAN, ON FRIDAY 16 NOVEMBER 1945 AT AROUND LUNCHTIME.

Demob leave, coupled with one extra day for each month served abroad, meant I would continue to receive pay for about the following three months. There was also a gratuity paid.

ISBN 141202651-2

Printed in Great Britain
by Amazon

26235539R00149